PAGAN GRACE

Dionysos, Hermes, and Goddess Memory in Daily Life

GINETTE PARIS

Translated from the French
by Joanna Mott

SPRING PUBLICATIONS, INC.
PUTNAM, CONNECTICUT

Published by Spring Publications, Inc.
28 Front Street, Suite 3
Putnam, CT 06260
www.springpublications.com

Distributed by The Continuum International Publishing Group
www.continuumbooks.com

Manufactured in Canada

Tenth Printing 2006

Cover design by white.room productions, New York

Lines from "Hymn to Hermes" quoted by permission of Noel Cobb as originally
published in *Harvest* (1986). Charles Boer gave permission for the quotations from
his translation of *The Bacchae* in *An Anthology of Greek Tragedy*, eds. A. Cook and E.
Dolin (Dallas: Spring Publications, Inc., 1983) and *The Homeric Hymns* (Dallas: Spring
Publications, Inc., 1979), © 1970, 1972 by Charles Boer.

Library of Congress Cataloging-in-Publication Data

Paris, Ginette
    Pagan grace : Dionysos, Hermes, and the goddess memory in daily life /
Ginette Paris ; translated from the French by Joanna Mott.
        p.   cm.
    Includes bibliographical references.
    ISBN 0-88214-342-5
    1. Dionysos (Greek deity) 2. Hermes (Greek deity) 3. Mnemosyne (Greek deity)
    4. Mythology, Greek—Psychological aspects.
I. Title.
BL820.B2P37   1990, 2003
292.2'11—dc20   89-26330
                                                                        CIP

⊗ The paper used in this publication meets the minimum requirements of the
American National Standard for Information Sciences — Permanence of Paper for
Printed Library Materials, ANSI Z39.48-1992.

Ce livre est dedié à Lune Maheu.

This book is dedicated to Lune Maheu.

CONTENTS

PART THREE *Goddess Memory* *117*

ACKNOWLEDGMENTS

Many people have supported me during the years I've spent writing this book, and I want to express my gratitude to all of them. I realize now, as I put the finishing touches to it, how much criticism, praise, discussion of ideas and exchange of comments are forms of love and friendship.

The historian Zenon-Gilles Maheu advised me in all matters relating to the history of ancient Greece and offered me his own erudition in abundance. Jeanne Bauer, a Jungian analyst, brought me interesting commentaries about Dionysos. My brother, Claude Paris, shared his experience as philosopher and writer. Claude Gagnon, a medievalist, guided me through the confusion of Hermetic alchemy and proved to me, each time we met, that ideas are the spice of life.

James Hillman read all my drafts carefully and on scribbled postcards or bits of yellow paper sent me several important ideas which bring out the psychological subtleties in Dionysos, Hermes and Mnemosyne. Under his tutelage I rediscovered a sympathetic feeling toward Ariadne and understood the more somber aspects of Dionysian psychology. He also agreed to go over the entire manuscript at the point when, having reread it too often, I could no longer render a judgment. His editor's pen and his lively spirit have reviewed the whole text and enhanced it in several places.

The last portion of Part One (on Dionysos) was given at the 1987 "Myth and Theatre" conference at the Château de Malé-rargues, France, and was published in *Sphinx 2: A Journal for Archetypal Psychology and the Arts* (1989).

I received financial aid and institutional support from the Conseil de Recherche en Sciences Humaines du Canada (CRSH), the

FCAR fund for University Research, and the publishing fund of the Vice-Rector of Communications at the University of Quebec at Montreal. The Department of Communications at my university, by granting me partial work-reduction, provided a moral and material atmosphere in which to do research. Colleagues like Marquita Riel and Roger Tessier, who were present at the very beginning of the work more than twelve years ago, provided the friendship and intellectual companionship that are terribly important just to survive and to publish in a university setting.

Sylvie Brouillette revised the French text and offered valuable stylistic advice. Joanna Mott, who did the English translation, showed great patience with my last-minute additions and helped me to believe in my own work by the care she applied to the work of translation. Mary Helen Sullivan revised the final text more than once with rare ability. Valery Beaugrand Champagne ran the necessary errands to libraries and bookstores to find the books we needed. Dany Beaupré of the J. A. de Sève Center of UQAM helped me in my occasionally tumultuous relationship with the microcomputer.

INTRODUCTION
The Gods and Goddesses

I love them as if they really existed, so inevitably someone will ask me, "Just how much do you *believe* in these pagan Gods and Goddesses?" I don't *believe* in them at all. No more but no less than I believe in the ego, the superego, the self, consciousness, unconsciousness, the Oedipus complex, Cassandra, Cinderella or Peter Pan; no more but no less than I believe in all the ideas invented by psychology to define inner dynamics: repression, regression, retrogression, progression, compensation, over-compensation, decompensation, depression, projection, introjection, retroflection, fusion, confusion, diffusion, transference, counter-transference, self-actualization, complexes, archetypes, individuation. None of that really exists either, does it? They're just more or less useful concepts and metaphors that allow us to grasp our inner life.

I am a social psychologist attached to a Department of Communications, and so we are thirty-six professors who devote ourselves to that capricious and invisible divinity, Communication. No one has ever seen it, it is no more present in "its" department than in any other, and yet we stay there, confident that there is such a thing as *Communication* and that this impalpable reality is worth devoting ourselves to. But why should the *concept* of communication be more credible or more useful than the Hermes image, which the ancients treated as if it were communication personified?

Abstract terms like communication, desire, power, reason, passion and the majority of concepts found in psychology textbooks describe invisible realities that the ancient Greeks evoked by giving them a personality and a name with a capital letter. They made them into divinities: instead of a theory of communication they had Hermes, instead of a theory of sexuality and a concept of libido they had Aphrodite, instead of seminars on organizational power they made up stories about Zeus's divine management. Where we have an engineering school, they had Apollo's disciples who were capable of constructing bridges more solid than ours. They didn't talk about the damaging effects of drugs but about the madness that Dionysos sends to anyone who refuses to honor him. They didn't develop a psychological theory on the nature of the mother–child connection, but they set to music and poetry the lamentations of Demeter separated from her daughter.

My need to return to the Gods and Goddesses has nothing to do with a new religious esoteric doctrine. First of all because it's psychology we're dealing with and not religion. Secondly, because it is precisely the use of an abstract and falsely precise vocabulary in scientific psychology that convinces me that we will gain by looking once again at the founding images, the ones behind the concepts which we use to try to understand ourselves.

Each mythical personage is valuable in itself, and it is not my intention to treat polytheistic imagery simply as a catalogue of models for behavior. When we consider the divinities' personified qualities we mustn't take them to be prescriptions, as if we were being asked to be as sensual as Aphrodite, as intelligent as Athena, as wily as Hermes. Archetypal psychology, on the contrary, sees itself as an antidote to a psychology that asks us to be everything at once, to be without psychological flaws, without symptoms, in the image of saints whom we imagine to be sinless and a God who rejects his own shadow, the devil. The pagan Gods attract me precisely because each one appears both perfect and incomplete, divine and demonic, both crazy and wise like the unconscious.

There are better authorities on the Greeks and better scholarly works on Dionysos, Hermes and Mnemosyne. I don't pretend to encompass their nature and capacity but rather to reflect their penetration. My intention in this book is to honor these three divinities from my own experience and life, relating the story of my encounter with them.

Goddess, sing to us about the exploits of the divinities, and may your muses grant me pagan grace.

PART ONE

Dionysos

Soul-making through the Body

> Oh how lucky you are, how really lucky you are,
> if you know the gods from within,
> if you're for clean living,
> if you get the feel of Bacchus
> and you do it in the hills
> pure in your soul,
> and to sit in on the orgies
> of Great Mother Cybele,
> to shake a wand in the air,
> to wear ivy on your head,
> to serve Dionysus, how lucky you are!
> Go Bacchae! oh go Bacchae!
>
> Euripides, *The Bacchae*

The face of a man on the edge of orgasm has piercing, enlarged eyes, congested with power, like those of an animal encountered at night. His face darkens, his neck veins swell, he goes mad. Sometimes he growls, pants, cries out. Dionysos lives again! The God who symbolizes the revenge of the forces of instinct over the forces of order is the Roarer, the Loud-Shouter, the Loosener, the Beast, the Mountain Bull.

The name *Bacchus* for Dionysos is inseparable in Greek from a verb meaning "to act like a Bacchant"—that is, to become agitated, to cry out, to fall into a trance, to act crazily. The ancient Greeks had a more extensive vocabulary than we do to describe trance and excitement. Translators have had trouble finding the words to describe that frenetic madness without falling into the vocabulary of pathology. But if scholars have tended to pathologize the Dionysian, it's not just because of a lack of words. It's because we've lost the connection to that archetype and, with it, the chance to let off steam without risking denigration as pathological freaks. The translators couldn't find words because "they saw hysteria in Dionysos rather than recognizing Dionysos in hysteria"![1]

As for the Christians, they couldn't make sense of a spirituality and an ecstasy attained through the body, so they transformed Dionysos-the-God into Dionysos-the-Devil. While it's true that *ekstasis* meant that the soul was liberated from its bodily attachment, it's also true that Dionysian ecstasy is reached through an *intensification of bodily feelings*. The adjective *Bromios*, which is frequently applied to Dionysos, can be translated by "noisy" but also, as Henri Jeanmaire suggests, by "shivering," "buzzing" or "trembling," which well suits the state of Dionysian excitation in which body and soul are mutually stirred.[2] Dionysian excess plunges into the nocturnal part of ourselves and the nocturnal part of life, in close proximity to what is organic, damp, and bloody.

This state of excitation, although primitive, is not so easy to attain; it's not enough to drink, eat, shout, dance or make love excessively to get to the point of Dionysian rapture. Why would the initiation into the Dionysian state be any less strewn with difficulties than the initiation into other archetypal figures? On the path toward Dionysian liberation we often run first into a torrent of emotional mud and bloody rage, instead of the anticipated ecstasy. Alcohol and psychotropic drugs, also under the patronage of Dionysos, can loosen tongues and open up the doors of perception, but they just as surely lead to destruction and paranoia.

Eat, Drink and Be Mad

Since Dionysos brings intensity, life without him is a bore and psychosomatic research has confirmed what the Maenads knew a long time ago: boredom and repression can kill you! Dionysos won't stand for us being governed only by the light of reason and everyday awareness: then he becomes the vengeful "bringer of madness."

In Greece the Dionysian festivals were associated with primitive feasts. The legend of the frenzied women in Dionysos's cortege has them tumbling down mountains, catching animals and devouring them raw.

> Oh how tremendous it is, when someone is in the hills
> and getting dizzy from all the fun
> and he falls on the ground and the fawnskin

falls over him while he was chasing the goat for its blood,
and because he likes raw meat,
all the way to the hills of Phrygia, or Lydia,
and Bromius is leading you, Evoi![3]

The thiasos was a country fair, combining feast and religious ritual, where each person brought a contribution in kind. Gastronomical rituals that require sophisticated service, formal dress, white linen and fragile china are just the opposite of the noisy, rustic and bucolic Dionysian feast. No one felt obligated to anyone else, because the thiases didn't depend on the generosity of a powerful or rich host. The fact that they took place in the countryside allowed for even more freedom and underscored the communal aspect of the feast. All feasts and banquets, however, are not thiases: there has to be a group emotion, a group enthusiasm for Dionysos.

One must not confuse Dionysian appetite with bulimia or chronic overeating; eating without appetite is anti-Dionysiac. That is why the thiasos was preceded by a fast. The God and his followers recovered their appetites by fasting, just as Aphrodite renewed her virginity by bathing in the sea. The image of a fat Bacchus stuffing himself passively is a decadent version of Dionysian pleasure that Christianity has given us, as if this pleasure were vulgar or sinful because the body is involved. Yet, a certain piggishness and gluttony—even greed—are part of Dionysian appetite, whether it be hunger for food or sexual hunger. For example, Gargantua and his wife Gargamelle, the characters described by Rabelais at the time of the Renaissance, are capable of every excess and yet are models of exuberance and mental health. In that they are Dionysian.

Sexual Appetite

The Dionysos who tears off chunks of juicy meat with his teeth, enjoys licking his fingers, and squirts wine from his flask sometimes approaches sexuality with the same rustic manners. This approach can be interpreted more as a sign of sexual appetite than as an expression of vulgarity or sexist violence. Dionysian sexuality does not have the subtlety of Aphrodisian sexuality, but the fact that Dionysos is a sexual figure in the same pantheon as Aphrodite means there is room for his kind of sexuality as well. Unfortunately, however, the sexual Dionysos was discredited along with the gourmand Dionysos. The image of the Satyrs with their goat legs and horns became one of the most popular representations of the Devil, though the Christians censored the erect penises and lewd smiles characteristic of these Dionysian companions. Whether as half-horse or half-goat, the pagan Satyr has an enormously large male organ, perpetually erect, and he is represented dancing through the countryside, drinking wine, chasing nymphs. The God Pan and the God Priapus, who were part of the Dionysian cult, are also represented with the legs, horns, and beard of a goat and an erect phallus pointing toward the sky. During the Dionysia, a giant phallus was paraded through the crowd as an expression of 'religious' fervor for the God. Legend says that Pan was so sexually active that, when he couldn't find a nymph or even a young shepherd to satisfy his lust, he invented masturbation.

Aphrodite and Dionysos are the two Greek divinities most often associated with sexuality, but in very different ways. When one thinks of Aphrodite, the image is graceful seductiveness, symbolized by the rose and the dove. A subtle choreography of gestures, both enticing and distancing, a feeling with the tonal quality of flute and rhythm as the sound of waves are hers, whereas Dionysos-the-Mountain-Bull underscores his erection with drums. He personifies the animal power of sexual need and the harshness with which desire can seize us, transforming us into Bacchants. It's Dionysos who makes us tear off our clothes (or at least pop our buttons), messes up our hair, knocks over things, and disturbs the neighbors.

Dionysos's sexual energy is powerful, deep-rooted, gutsy, making us drink at the very source of animal life. Sometimes the very strength of Dionysian sexual desire can make us lose contact with the other person. We are then completely identified with the intensity of our feelings and sensations and lose sight of the humanity of our partner: Dionysos possesses us completely. If the partner is not as high, as possessed by Dionysos, he or she might feel scorched by the intensity of the emotional and sexual discharge. We could call that the "Semele syndrome": Semele, Dionysos's mother, was wasted and burned by the intense radiance of her divine lover. Here is the story as I interpret it.

Dionysos is the child of Zeus and a mortal, Semele, one of the four daughters of King Cadmos, founder of Thebes. In order to seduce Semele, Zeus takes on the appearance of a human, but insists that he is the supreme God of Olympus, Zeus in person! Semele is persuaded and becomes pregnant by him.

But Hera, his legitimate spouse and queen of Olympus, is not a Goddess to overlook such an affront. In turn, she assumes a human form, that of Semele's nurse, in order to talk to the young woman. "Really, you believed that handsome lover who pretends he's a God? You're very naive, my dear, and now you're pregnant. The next time he visits you, ask him for some proof. If he's really the all-powerful Zeus, let him show himself in all his splendor!" Thinking her wise old nurse is speaking to her, Semele begins to suspect that she has been deceived by an ordinary man.

At her lover's next visit, Semele asks Zeus if he would grant her a favor. "Sure, anything! I give you my word I will grant you any favor!" says Zeus. "Then, drop your human disguise and show yourself all-powerful," says Semele. Zeus warns her of the danger, but to no avail. Since he has given his word, he grants her wish. But Semele is not a Goddess, and so she cannot bear the intensity of light that emanates from her divine partner; she falls, struck down by light.

The child she carries is threatened, and to allow the fetus to continue its growth, Zeus hastens to graft it into his thigh which he then closes with golden clamps. When the gestation period is over, Illythia, the Goddess of childbirth, helps Zeus to open the clamps and give birth to the infant Dionysos, the "twice-born."

The image can be used as a sexual metaphor: one can easily imagine how the orgasm of the master of thunder and lightning would be too strong for a human partner! Like Semele, one can be psychologically burned by the radiance of one's lover, burned in relationships that give us more than we can handle, burned by the very intensity of feelings. Equilibrium in the intensity of feelings is not only important for comfort; it might be a precaution to avoid Semele's destiny: to become a cool, shadowy figure in the realm of Hades, emotionally burned out, sexually exhausted, socially scarred.

Orgy, Orgy, Orgy . . .

The Dionysian is often thought to be linked to a collective, convivial kind of sexuality. Anthropologists and historians have described a variety of collective sexual practices in many different societies. Whether it be the practice of exchanging wives, the ideology of free love, the licence of carnivals, or the sexual frenzy of Dionysian celebrations, collective sexuality is a constant in human history. The French sociologist Michel Maffesoli shows that what he calls "orgyism" is not only permanent but also necessary for the social fabric to maintain itself. Without a certain amount of "sharing of bodies," the mechanism of attraction, the connection, the "glue" that holds a community together might break down.[4] Maffesoli goes back to Emile Durkheim's concepts to describe how passion provides a reservoir of energy which insures the continuance of the social structure, even in modern societies which appear to be hyper-rationalistic.

Originally, the word *orgy* meant a religious event recognized by the authorities. A Dionysian orgy was therefore a form of Dionysos-worship, accepted as such by the city. But the nocturnal aspect of some Dionysian celebrations, the dissipation brought about by wine, by dancing and music, the presence of women "possessed" by their God—all this was responsible for the connotation of debauchery later associated with the word *orgy*. Dionysos is part of what Gilbert Durand calls "night-mode"[5] —that is, a nocturnal consciousness associated with the moon, moisture, women, sexuality, emotions, the body and the earth, as opposed to "day-mode" connected to the sun, dryness, all that is rational and Apollonian. Durand explains from an anthropological point of view, as did the feminists from a political and psychological point of view, how the balance between the two is fundamental for every culture. If any given culture receives only Apollonian sunshine, it dries up and dies; conversely, if it receives too much Dionysian moisture, it rots and becomes crazy. A hyper-technologized, hyper-rationalized society is as crazy, in a way, as is an anti-intellectual rock 'n roll subculture. We need both Dionysos and Apollo.

The Eleusinian Mysteries

Not only does Dionysos reflect back to us the sexual imagery of our culture, he also brings up images associated with altered states of consciousness induced by alcohol, psychotropic drugs, or dances. Dionysos-Bacchus is still known today as the patron saint of drinkers; most cities have a bar or a restaurant called "Bacchus," usually decorated with frescoes full of wine vats, baskets of grapes, and chubby-cheeked fellows with red noses. Still, Greek wines seem to have been of a particular sort: three little cups of undiluted wine were enough to take one to the edge of madness! Some wines were diluted by water twenty to one. If, unfortunately, the drinker didn't take the precaution of diluting his wine, he ran the risk of brain damage and even death.

The anthropologist Gordon Wasson, along with the ethnobotanist Carl Ruck and the chemist Albert Hofmann (who discovered LSD), has focused attention on the Greek custom of diluting wine, because he sees in it a paradox.[6] In fact, the art of distillation wasn't known to the Greeks, so their wine could not have had an alcohol content of more than fourteen percent. We also know that their most common drink, mead, was made by fermenting a mixture of water and honey in the sun, which cannot produce results as powerful as those attributed to wine. How do we reconcile these facts with the many descriptions of the delirious effects that wine had on the Greeks? This apparent contradiction can be resolved, according to the three researchers, by the fact that the wine of Greek antiquity—as is true of the wines of most ancient peoples—was a mixture of infusions and toxins in a winy drink. Unguents and spices and herbs with psychotropic properties could be added at the ritual moment of diluting the wine with water. When the ancient Greek invoked Dionysos as the God of wine, under the name of Bacchus, he had in mind a guide to other states of consciousness through psychotropic drugs as well as the patron saint of happy tipplers.

Every culture has its mind-altering drinks and drugs, but at the same time it creates social structures to deal with them. In Western culture wine is associated with gastronomy, with celebration and sociability, its purpose being to loosen tongues and dissolve social inhibitions. We learn how to deal with someone who occasionally goes on a bender and drinks too much. The laws against driving a vehicle while under the influence of alcohol don't condemn temporary drunkenness, only the error in judgment of someone who doesn't realize that you can't invoke Bacchus for reliable reflexes on the road. The destructive effects of alcohol on the American Indians at the beginning of colonization, or the damage it brings to Arab cultures when it is introduced abruptly, can be compared to the way the West has dealt with the power of LSD, hallucinogenic mushrooms, and hashish. Alcoholism and drug addiction are not Dionysian revelries that go on too long; they are failures in our encounter with Dionysos, failures to acknowledge what he stands for, failures to understand his guidance.

Adolescents who get stoned on drugs, as the American Indians once got drunk on alcohol, are unaware of the true power of their substance, just as they are unaware of its evil effects. What they are looking for is Dionysos. What they are offered is an overdose of all sort of drugs in the absence of a guiding spirit. Encounter with the Dionysos who opens the chemical doors of perception asks for a ritual that holds in check and formalizes, a community that gives it meaning. From the perspective of the ancient Greeks, we might say that through our teenagers, our drug addicts and our alcoholics, we suffer the vengeance of a God to whom we refuse true Dionysia and whose mysteries, once celebrated at Eleusis, no longer have any equivalent. Without an experienced guide and without any kind of ritual, the initiation into the power of any psychotropic drug can only be traumatic. We do not learn when, how, where, with whom to take drugs, and we fail to avoid the most obvious pitfalls. Most of all, we do not learn when *not* to take them.

True Dionysia cannot be planned like a nocturnal picnic with a supply of hashish and a basket of food and drinks. Dionysia must emerge from a culture or a community, and the preparation must be psychological as well as practical, personal as well as collective, mundane as well as spiritual. The counterculture years have been a long Dionysian eruption for a whole generation. The embers of old Dionysos were smoldering; it was enough to blow on them to cause a great fire. But these Dionysia are long gone, and our culture does not offer them very often.

The team of Wasson, Ruck and Hofmann has focused its research on the scene at Eleusis, near Athens, and analyzed the receptacles which were reported to have been used at the celebrated Mysteries, where Demeter and Dionysos were honored by a secret initiatory rite. This secret (of women at its beginning) was surely one of the best kept in history, contrary to the saying that a woman cannot hold a secret. We still don't know exactly what the famous Eleusinian Mysteries were about, even though they were already established in the Bronze Age and continued through the rationalism of classical Greece up to the point when Christianity suppressed them. Pilgrims went to the sanctuary at Eleusis in search of revelation, of initiation into a vision of eternity. Anyone—man, woman, slave or emperor—could be initiated at Eleusis except the Barbarians, that is, anyone not Greek. In the Hellenic and Roman era this restriction disappeared, and the Mysteries prevailed over the entire civilized world. In the face of Christianity, Eleusis remained one of the major centers of pagan resistance, right up to the end.

Dionysos was not represented at Eleusis at the beginning of the Mysteries, which belonged principally to Demeter (or Cybele or Gaia, other Mother-Goddesses). The basic image of the Mysteries remained that of the Mother separated from her daughter Persephone who has been carried off by Hades. The Mother, inconsolable and angry, wanders over the earth. When the Mother is angry life is barren: as long as her daughter is not returned, Demeter refuses to play her role as Goddess of Fertility. Winter symbolizes the ensuing period of sterility.

Still looking for her daughter, Demeter, in tears, arrives one day at Eleusis disguised as a poor old woman and is greeted by the people and their king Keleos who offer her hospitality. She meets there another old woman, Baubo, who distracts her briefly from her pain by making her laugh at some jokes. The story goes that old Baubo lifted up her dress to show Demeter her wrinkled backside while tossing off all sorts of obscenities. Baubo is so funny that Demeter forgets her sorrow and laughs with the old woman.

That episode with old Baubo is taken up again in the Eleusinian ritual when everyone yells obscenities as the procession advances—as if to remind us that laughing is part of the divine. As so often happens in our lives, humor is the beginning of the end of Demeter's rigid stance; from then on, she moves to rage. Rage and humor are fundamental psychological moves that can help us out of depression: to laugh at oneself or at a funny situation is a sure sign that one is coming out of the inferiority feeling, out of one's egocentric preoccupation. To laugh is to take a distance, and to gain perspective one has to move out of the depressive pit.

Zeus realizes that he has to yield to Demeter's rage in order to preserve life itself. He gives back the daughter so that the curse of sterility may be lifted. Symbolically this is spring: the meeting of mother and daughter. Mother and daughter will be together and happy for some months: this is summer. When Persephone returns to her husband Hades, we have autumn and winter again. Joyful to find her daughter, Demeter remembers the welcome she received at Eleusis and repays its people by giving them the gift of agriculture and the privilege of being initiated into the Mysteries. Good King Keleos's son, Triptoleme, becomes the first propagator of grain and a hero of the Goddess.

Herodotus mentions that the ceremonies marking the autumnal separation of mother from daughter were initially reserved for married women: the Thesmophoria took place in October (the time to sow) and lasted three days. Only women could participate in the Thesmophoria since they did the sowing. In the ritual the seed was mixed with menstrual blood, which was considered not as some impure and maleficent substance but as a symbol of the feminine power of fertility. Mixing the grain with menstrual blood was believed to strengthen its power to germinate. The Great Mysteries, like the ancient Thesmophoria, took place in autumn, at the end of August or beginning of September, while the Lesser Mysteries in February celebrated the reunion between mother and daughter.

The Great Mysteries were one of the largest festivals in all Greece. The residents of Eleusis (where the Mysteries, strictly speaking, were held) and those of Athens hosted the initiates as well as the mystae (candidates for initiation). On the first day, the young Athenians marched solemnly to Demeter's temple at Eleusis to accompany the priestesses who carried the sacred vases. They brought the vases back to Athens and placed them in a sanctuary at the foot of the Acropolis, a place called the Eleusinion. The true celebration began the following day when the mystae, called together by the hierophant, high priest of the Mysteries, went down to the sea for a purifying bath. Afterward an impressive procession formed with priests and priestesses carrying the sacred objects, followed by high Athenian officials, young ephebes, and finally the mystae and a crowd of onlookers. The magnificent procession moved slowly along the Sacred Way between Athens and Eleusis, with many stops at sanctuaries along the route (one was the place where Baubo had met Demeter). A statue of Iacchus, the mystical name for Dionysos as companion of the Mother-Goddess, was carried along in the cortege.

There were two stages, two levels of initiation at Eleusis. The first-degree initiation involved a communion with bread (also called "cakes") and a drink, the *kykeon*. The second-degree initiation could require up to a year of probation. Only the initiates of the second level participated in the High Mysteries which culminated in the union of the High Priest with the High Priestess. This liturgical drama symbolized the sacred union of archetypal Man and Woman, from whom the Child was born. The drama was a celebration of the eternal mystery of love and the renewal of life.

Originally, the Mysteries were a cult of the Mother-Goddess to whom the spouse or consort was sacrificed (literally or symbolically). The intensification of patriarchal values is responsible for the gradual decrease in the importance of the Goddess figure and the enhancement of the role of Dionysos as spouse. But as long as the Mysteries have lasted, one central image has remained: the initiate, whether man or woman, identifies with the Goddess, rather than the God, and "feels" life, love, and cyclic time through the image of the mother-daughter eternal chain of being.

The Revelation

According to Hofmann, who analyzed the substance found by scraping the sacred vases used at Eleusis, the chemical structure of the communion drink, the *kykeon*, contained a hallucinogenic drug derived from ergot, a microscopic mushroom that develops on grain. Moreover, this chemical structure strangely resembles that of LSD 25. Hofmann's chemical demonstration that the transformation of personality undergone by the Eleusinian initiate was encouraged by a hallucinogenic drink is supported by arguments and data assembled by his colleagues Wasson and Ruck, who drew from botany, history, ethnography and mythology. The physical symptoms described as preceding the Eleusinian vision are similar to those induced by LSD 25: fear, trembling, nausea, cold sweats. Then comes the experience described as a vision of a brilliant aureole rising out of a dark cavern.

To those who explore the caverns of consciousness through psychotropic drugs, it may be pointed out that the initiate only went to Eleusis once or twice in his or her whole life. The overall preparation—fasts, purifications, instruction and teachings prior to initiation—could last up to a year, during which the mystae had to stay near Eleusis where the priests and priestesses acted like therapists-guides-professors. The opinion of Hofmann, the scientist who discovered LSD, might also be of interest:

> In common parlance, among the many who have not experienced ecstasy, ecstasy is fun, and I am frequently asked why I do not reach for mushrooms every night. But ecstasy is not fun. Your very soul is seized and shaken until it tingles. . . . The unknowing vulgar abuse the word, and we must recapture its full and terrifying sense.[7]

The initiate of Eleusis became "a person-who-knows-without-needing-words." Liturgical songs and rhythm were heard, but no tradition reports a discourse of any kind. The etymology of the word *mystery* relates to a word meaning "to be silent." The initiates were there to learn to experience new states of consciousness, to acquire an intimate knowledge of the immortality of the soul, endlessly born again in other forms. Plutarch, mourning the loss of his daughter, writes to his wife as follows, summoning up their shared experience at Eleusis to allay his grief.

> About that which you have heard, dear heart, that the soul once departed from the body vanishes and feels nothing, I know that you give no belief to such assertions because of those sacred and faithful promises given in the mysteries of Bacchus which we who are of that religious brotherhood know. We hold it firmly for an undoubted truth that our soul is incorruptible and immortal. We are to think (of the dead) that they pass into a better place and a happier condition. Let us behave ourselves accordingly, outwardly ordering our lives, while within all should be purer, wiser, incorruptible. . . .[8]

The celebrated secret of Eleusis couldn't be revealed through words, for it was essentially an experiential path which led to a level of knowledge that cannot be verbally expressed. Eleusis couldn't talk about itself any more than therapy can talk about itself. Even when one tries to describe the therapeutic process, the listener usually ends up bored because this process has to be lived to be understood. The merely curious ("what the hell are you doing in those therapy sessions?"), even when told, are disappointed.

The greatest mysteries—like love, inner visions, "insights"—are often simple ones. If they seem esoteric to the uninitiated, it is not out of deception or intention to hide but because words are powerless to account for them. It is like trying to explain to a child what it is to make love. One usually ends up saying, "You'll see, when you are a grown-up. . . ." At this point, we sense the difference between Dionysian consciousness, emotional and experiential, and Apollonian consciousness, which is abstract and formal.

Bringer of Madness

Dionysos brings madness to King Lycurgus and to his cousin King Pentheus, because they won't recognize his divinity. The story is worth telling. One can read it as a fable about the danger of having an exclusively rationalistic point of view on life.

To protect the baby Dionysos from Hera's rage, Zeus gives him to the nymphs of legendary Mount Nysa, telling them to dress him as a girl so that Hera will not find him. These nurse-nymphs care for him and raise him, with occasional help from Silenus, an old Satyr who becomes his tutor. At adolescence Dionysos discovers wine, and as his virility asserts itself his girlish disguise becomes less and less plausible. Hera finds him, and at that moment he goes mad. The myth doesn't say whether his madness comes from Hera's vengeance, from too much wine, or from the crisis of adolescence itself, but states simply that in his madness he wanders across Greece, Egypt and Syria.

When he reaches Phrygia, he is welcomed by the great Goddess Cybele whom the Phrygians also call Mother of the Gods, or Great Mother, and whose powers extend to all the forces of vegetation. She greets young Dionysos, purifies him, initiates him into the ritual of her cult and cures him of his madness. This encounter with the Goddess marks a turning point, because from now on

Dionysos, who is only a half-God since he was born of a mortal, undertakes a long voyage of conquest which will eventually make him an Olympian God. The myth is no more precise about his cure than it is about what drove him to madness: is it because he is freed of his madness that he achieves divinity, or is it because Cybele convinces him of his divinity that he is cured? Who can say what is cause and what is effect? However it is, at this moment the young God reaches Thrace and begins his religious conquests.

In Thrace King Lycurgus is not impressed with this young man who thinks he's a God and tries to imprison him. But there's always a woman, a nymph or a Goddess to come to Dionysos's rescue. This time it's Thetis, the Goddess of the seas, who protects him. Later, emboldened by Thetis, Dionysos will take vengeance on Lycurgus and drive him mad. Thinking he is destroying Dionysos's vine stock, King Lycurgus takes an axe and cuts off the limbs of his own son. The people, land and animals of his kingdom become sterile. The oracle, consulted about this calamity, reveals that the fault is the king's refusal to recognize the divinity of the new God and that only his death will avenge Dionysos and restore fertility. The Thracians tear their king apart by tying him to four horses which gallop off in four directions, and they proclaim the divinity of Dionysos.

He continues his journey toward India in a chariot drawn by black panthers, accompanied by a cortege acclaiming him a triumphant God. When he reaches the Ganges, he turns around and retraces his steps, gloriously returning to Greece, to Boetia, the homeland of his mother, princess of the city of Thebes. There, Euripides tells us, he must confront his grandfather, old Cadmos, and his cousin Pentheus, to whom Cadmos has given power. There's also his aunt Agave, Pentheus's mother and sister to his mother Semele. Dionysos arrives in his home town accompanied by the Bacchants, the disheveled women of his cortege. They sing and dance excitedly, beating on drums. Some, according to legend, tame venomous snakes that nest in their hair and dance on their heads during the processions. The motley crowd moves through the city, inciting the Theban matrons to drop their housework and join the Bacchanalia, which is celebrated at night in the mountains with dancing, singing and wine.

Pentheus does not approve: he hates disorder and nocturnal celebrations and rituals that send women into mystical delirium.

He confronts Dionysos and tries to stop the proceedings. But Agave, Pentheus's mother, is drawn into the Bacchanalia and Dionysos strikes her with madness. Thinking he is well hidden, Pentheus spies on the women. They seize him, mistaking him for a wildcat, and tear him apart. Dionysos once again avenges the refusal to honor his divinity.

He then travels toward the isle of Naxos, setting off with a group of pirates who are willing to take him aboard but unwilling to believe his divinity. Since he's a handsome young man, they plan to sell him as a slave. Dionysos sees through their ruse and transforms their oars into serpents, grows an enormous ivy to encircle the boat tightly and a magic vine to climb the mast and overrun the sails. What's more, he induces hallucinations in the pirates of wild animals swarming into the boat. Beside themselves with terror, the sailors jump into the sea, where they are transformed into dolphins. To this day dolphins follow ships and show affection for sailors, for they are themselves repentant mariners.

Madness was often perceived by the Greeks as a punishment of Dionysos. If we can judge by the way he punished Lycurgus, or Pentheus, or the pirates who carried him to Naxos, Dionysos can't bear people who value reason and moderation above all else, who repress all grunts, spasms of laughter and tears, those naive enough to think they can rid themselves of all darkness, of all madness. In psychological language, "contempt for Dionysos" can be translated as a "repression of instincts," whereas a "punishment of Dionysos" is a neurosis or a psychosis.

In reaction to a model of mental health that has been for so long anti-Dionysian and feeling the Dionysian winds coming from the counterculture of the sixties, the British psychiatrists Ronald Laing and David Cooper called themselves anti-psychiatrists and presented madness, not as a symptom to be eliminated, but as a fever which fights the illness, part of a larger process of search for mental balance. They proposed replacing the "debasement ceremony" as one enters the asylum with an "initiation ceremony" providing those undertaking this voyage into madness with the conditions necessary to assure a round-trip.[9] This approach was enthusiastically received by the counterculture. Some took it as an invitation to search for madness, to plumb the depths, to descend into the underworld, with the hope of coming out free and clear. However, anti-psychiatry was still linked with the institution, offering the schizophrenics a home and professional guidance for their trip into madness.

At the same period, humanistic psychologists tried to avoid the term *madness*. Less interested in schizophrenics, they labeled their approach a "therapy for the normal" and validated the Dionysian in the form of "peak experiences," emotional or sexual paroxysms, radical and creative lifestyles for "inner-directed" personalities.

Other approaches derivative of Wilhelm Reich and the bio-energetics of Alexander Lowen integrated physical exercises into the therapeutic agenda, giving value to the bodily expression of emotion. These approaches acted as an antidote to the almost exclusive importance given to formal and mental Apollonian expression in traditional psychoanalysis. The profusion and differentiation of "body therapies" make it difficult to examine them as a whole, but their common focus is on expressed and intensive communication, the language of Dionysos.[10]

Psychological Dismemberment

Whatever the approach, all agree that it's one thing to be in touch with one's madness and another to become insane. Dionysos invites us in the dark night of the psyche, pushes us into the depths of the cavern, but the going is often easier than coming back: the initiation into the Mysteries was something one didn't take lightly. When intensities turn to horror, Dionysos can be heard in groans of agony and screams of pain. Madness that is a punishment of Dionysos has nothing romantic about it; it destroys and it hurts. In her madness the Bacchant Agave no longer recognizes her son and, mistaking him for a wildcat, tears off his limbs. Pentheus dies dismembered.

But she was foaming at the mouth and her eyes were rolling around
  in her head like a crazy woman, and she was completely out of her
    mind,
a woman possessed by Bacchus, not thinking of her son,
and she grabbed his left arm at the wrist
and placed her foot against his ribs, the poor thing,
and then she tore his shoulder off,

not by her own strength, of course,
the god put that power in her hands. . . .[11]

Her reason restored, Agave understands that the dismemberment of her son is her own doing: *"Dionysus destroyed us all, only
now do I understand it."*[12] Dionysos destroys Pentheus through his
mother, Agave, because Pentheus refuses to make room for him in
a kingdom so well controlled it has become deadly. The destruction Dionysos has wrought on Thebes gives it a new life.

Though it is risky to deny the Dionysian, the opposite is just as
dangerous: the desire to equal Dionysos in intensity is taking
oneself as the equivalent of a divinity. It is psychological inflation.
People who seek out every possible reaction for its powerful emotions and exaggerate every emotion into paroxysms misjudge their
psychic strength, and ours. Instead of finding Dionysian intensity,
they feel an emptiness, as if their inner fiber had been worn out.
They have been burned up like Dionysos's mother, Semele. Too
much is too much. Their insatiable hunger for emotion and intense
experiences eventually brings the opposite of what they want;
nothing much is felt in their presence. Dionysos excites or invites
the Titanic element of excess in others. A person under the influence of Dionysos will drain out the Titanic excess in our own
behavior. Even the scholars and researchers become "excessive"
when talking about Dionysos. But one must not confuse intensity
and dismemberment. One feels exhausted, worn out, "shredded"
by the behavior of others who are so excited. Their wild orgiastic
drama becomes demanding. No more the generous Dionysian
–Demeterian cornucopia of life's flowing intensity.

What Jung called "identification with the archetype" is taking
the divinity inside oneself instead of being held in it. When identified with the archetype, one believes in one's own rhetoric,
justifies oneself within a closed mythology. The inflation specific
to Dionysos is intensity. Those who exercise this tyranny of intensity over us make us feel that we draw back from climax, that our
emotions are too controlled, that we're ordinary, lacking in
strength and passion, not vivacious enough, not emotional
enough, not excited enough, not enough . . . not enough. . . . They
measure other people on the superhuman scale of the archetype,
which is unfair! The true Dionysian personality communicates

intensity, while the person who is inflated by the Dionysian archetype is begging for it.

This exaggeration through an archetype always has disastrous results, no matter what the archetype is. The woman who "thinks she's Aphrodite," for example, makes people around her feel clumsy, lacking in grace, as if she can never be given enough attention, approached with enough subtlety, whereas the true Aphrodisian personality radiates a charm that sheds a golden light to all those around and makes them appear their best. The former believes she is the mistress of a power, while the latter *serves* the archetypal power of Beauty and Attraction. To shut oneself in a frigid narcissism is the exact opposite of the Aphrodisian spirit of generosity. The personality "inflated" by the Aphrodisian archetype takes for herself the love and respect that the man addresses, through the human woman, to the archetypal Woman, to the Goddess Aphrodite.

By the same token, the intellectual who "takes himself for Apollo" doesn't realize at what point his sophisticated jargon becomes an obstacle to intellectual clarity. In his company, we feel suddenly stupid, we can't understand what he's talking about, we suspect his expert language isn't entirely justified by the complexity of the subject, and so we end up mistrusting intellectual reasoning itself as if it were a weapon to dominate others. He doesn't shed light on the subject, as a true Apollonian would do; he turns the spotlight on himself. As a professor I have often noticed that those students who have a poor opinion of their own intellect submit to this kind of domination, and the less they understand the more they applaud. A true intellectual is the servant of ideas, while the caricature of Apollonian qualities expresses itself in mere academic verbiage. Inflation through an archetype makes us lose the very quality with which we identify too exclusively. In Greek mythology there are many warnings: don't try to match a divinity, ever!

Where societies have allowed them, Dionysias have always been well-defined in time, like a break in the daily routine, as if to underscore the exceptional quality of the moment which cannot and should not last. Jean-Jacques Wunenburger points out that, when the celebration claims to go on forever, it becomes meaningless and is only a complacent exploration of a thrill, losing its sacred dimension. Play must be an interval, a rest, an opening, a balance between the tension of performance and the violence of play.[13] Dionysias as an endless party become like those commercials that are ever more creative, more appealing, more imaginative, but to sell what? The God is left out.

The constant and willful pursuit of emotion and intensity falsifies human identity. It's a monotheistic view of Dionysos, which leads to a dull emptiness rather than to the throbbing heart of life. Dionysos is an earth God; no soil can be fertile that is not in constant relationship with the environment. Emotion that feeds on itself instead of being connected to the situation is quickly exhausted. It does not lead to an enthusiastic sharing; it's in fact a claim of the will on our emotions and is no longer Dionysian. To know Dionysos, one must open up to emotion, to the senses, to the tragic or comic aspects of life. Dionysos is an opening, a happening, not an organizing!

Participation

Apollo teaches us distance, while Dionysos teaches us proximity, contact, intimacy with ourselves, nature, and others. I knew a sociology professor, a typically Apollonian type who could no longer step out of his critical attitude toward social phenomena. He complained of always being at a distance, of having lost the knack of coming together with anything. He could analyze but never participate, and he feared he would end up becoming bitter. He stopped enjoying brilliant analyses of social events (lived by others); he had enough of his own biting irony. His drinking was sad, his sex life boring. He wanted spontaneity, participation, being part of something, but couldn't allow himself to dissolve into a group emotion. He knew all too well that the loss of critical function leads to the alienation of freedoms based on the ability to discriminate. But this knowledge kept him from enjoying the gifts of Dionysos that he secretly yearned for.

One summer day, after many weeks of supplication from his ten-year-old daughter, he took her to one of those giant water-slides. Of course, he had brought books and magazines to read while she played, and of course he thought water-slides a stupid, vulgar, promiscuous activity. He couldn't read: too much noise and too much insistence from his daughter that he should come with her, sit on a large rubber tube, and slide with it down the water-slide. He did. And, just there and then, he met Dionysos. The sliding, the acceleration and the final splash in the water pool—all this was felt as a sudden *coming into his body.* He was enraptured. For the first time in years he began to play, really play in the water, hear the joyous shouting of children and adults, feel the sun on his wet body. He didn't mind the proximity of so many half-naked bodies swimming around; he had images of wild horses splashing in a water pool and even liked the feeling of being one animal among others. His social persona was gone, and the suspension of critical functioning let him at last have a feeling of Dionysian participation.

Certainly, the sociology professor is right to be cautious: if the disappearance of critical functioning proves to be a permanent and collective choice, emotion is transferred to the emotions and values of a leader, and the sect phenomenon results. A sect has an intense group emotion around which the collective identity is built. There will then inevitably ensue an alienating polarization between, on the one hand, the irrational sect members and, on the other hand, those rationalists who become ever colder and more distant as the excitement grows. For both the Dionysian spirit is lost. The first group is convinced it's more "alive" than the other, while having renounced an important part of its freedom, whereas the second group rejects all Dionysian experience for fear of compromising its freedom of judgment and critical faculty.

The rather jolly figure of the Roman Bacchus to which we're accustomed, along with the Rousseauian aspect of humanistic psychology, has made us forget that the expression of "primitive" and "natural" passions is not an innocent process, no more than childhood is innocent. The desire to free oneself from the dictatorship of reason has more than once given birth to the most demoralizing sects and to an anti-intellectualism as alienating as the rationalistic denial of Dionysos. But the solution is not to be found by ignoring Dionysos; a polytheistic psychology allows one to respect Dionysos *and* Apollo.

Dionysos the Liberator

Walter F. Otto points out to what extent Dionysos's character is torn by contradiction.[14] Supportive and devouring, friendly and diabolical, meditative and excessive, Dionysos is just as paradoxical with regard to political values, for he is sometimes a liberator and sometimes a tyrant. He appears wherever revolution and revolt break out, but revolution is itself the height of contradiction between love and hate, celebration and massacre, destructive orgy and the elevation of noble ideals.

Revolutionary intensity is incarnated in charismatic leaders who incite us to seek total and immediate freedom, but this "madness" is applauded. Under their influence we break away from the ties, groups, institutions and people who constrain us. The need to destroy old forms is satisfied along with the need to celebrate together a long-awaited D-Day. Like any revolutionary leader who recruits his men from among those who have nothing to lose, Dionysos finds his Maenads among women who can't stand any longer being locked into the domestic enclosure. They become wild women who break their chains in order to follow Dionysos the Liberator.

It's not just tired and frustrated housewives who beseech Dionysos. When the prospect of following our career plan is so gloomy that we feel we may dry up on the dead tree of some bureaucracy, we yearn for him with the same feelings as those of the young Greek housewife bound to the loom all winter or those of the modern housewife bound to the vacuum cleaner and trapped in the feminine mystique. Today the risk of dying of boredom is less visible than that of dying of a heart attack or cancer, but boredom and suffocating rage under oppressive circumstances are nonetheless killers. That's when Dionysos's destructiveness takes on survival value; Dionysos the Liberator is called whenever there is a revolution, be it collective or personal. I know an old woman who says about someone she thinks too submissive or joyless "*she (or he) hasn't been through her revolution yet*" or "*here is a chance to make your revolution, dear*"—meaning that the person has relationships or situations in her life that need to be broken through, destroyed, destructured, deconstructed. For that, one needs Dionysos's violence. But where will he strike?

The place of the Dionysian seizure is precisely where one is most guarded against the God:

> If, for example, one has been raised to be "good" according to any tradition with ingrained standards of decorum/decency/dignity (all related to *dogma*), the seizure would occur in exactly those places where doctrinal decency is maintained. Foundations of identity tremble when the edifice is shaken. If marriage edifies, if a person's moral identity is tied up with "that forge upon which character is melded," then it is marriage that trembles when Dionysos approaches. If it is a career that builds strength of character, the discipline begins to waver. If it is power that edifies, one's sovereignty crumbles.[15]

But Dionysos-Liberator doesn't come without Dionysos-Tyrant. Everyone knows that the Monday morning collective hangover after D-Day can be a terrible letdown. The damage has to be cleaned up, and a part of what has been shattered by frenzy has to be rebuilt. It's at this moment of restoring routine that yesterday's liberator is transformed into a tyrant and sits in the seat of the one he has dislodged. Historians usually interpret this transformation from revolutionary to tyrant as a "corruption" of the revolution. Revolutionary imagination seems to include the belief that the tyranny-of-the-morning-after can, could, should have been avoided. But it is difficult to call an accident what is regularly repeated with each revolution. If the charismatic leader becomes a tyrant, it's perhaps because he enjoys a relationship with the governed that forgives him everything. The tyrants of ancient Greek or Renaissance Italian cities, as well as Napoleon Bonaparte, Stalin, Mao or Castro—all popular leaders but not democratic ones—were enthusiastically received as liberators because they had overturned the existing order. The sixth-century B.C. Greeks who led a revolt against the aristocracy called themselves liberators, claimed Dionysos as inspiration and became tyrants. This is why Werner Jaeger presents the tyrant as both a liberator, on the side of the people against the aristocracy, and as a charismatic despot who gives the people a lot of amusements, as long as they go along with the new rule.[16]

Dionysos was one of the people's favorite divinities (along with Aphrodite, Hermes, and Demeter), and the Greek tyrants who derived their power from the people took care to revive and to virtually institutionalize the Dionysian cult. Pisistratus, tyrant of Athens in the second half of the sixth century B.C., introduced the cult of Dionysos in the city (it was until then an agrarian cult) by instituting the Great Urban Dionysia, an addition to the rural one. Greek theater was born from these great Athenian Dionysia; these celebrations maintained the tyrant's popularity by giving the people the illusion of participation. Going to the theater was a great collective event, and the plays were much discussed. Many historians have noted the democratic quality of the Greek theater: in contrast to the cults of Zeus and Apollo (preferred Gods of the aristocrats), the Dionysian theater entertained everyone. Women, slaves, aliens, prisoners released for the occasion—all were invited to sit in the tiers and express their appreciation with cries, gestures, applause or protests. But this feeling of equality in the theater was counterbalanced by oppression from the outside.

The same pattern of evolution—from aristocracy to tyranny to democracy—was repeated in several Greek cities in the sixth century B.C. The tyrant freed the people from domination by the aristocracy and then established an autocracy. It was only when the power of the tyrant himself was questioned that democracy became possible. Most historians see this as a normal progression toward political maturity, but it can also be seen as confirmation of an archetypal constant: the Dionysos Liberator, the savior, doesn't come without his shadow, the tyrant. Not all tyrants—whether political, domestic or organizational—go as far as Dionysos, Tyrant of Syracuse, who presented himself as an incarnation of the God Dionysos, but each in his way knows how to convince people that, after the revolutionary struggle, all they have to do is trust him and let him decide what is best for them. Some tyrants remain in our memory as benefactors, as saviors; others turn out to be exploiters and are remembered negatively. But the first aren't less tyrannical than the second; they just hold on to the affection and trust of the people throughout their autocratic reign.

We may well ask what there is about our collective unconscious that feeds this archetype of a revolutionary, law-breaking, destructive God. Why does human society secrete its own destruction? Why can't we function like the complex society of ants, where one member would never think of destroying another's nest? Why do we have this God who regularly disrupts the social order and psychological tranquility? Revolutionaries cannot be classed as psychopaths or mutants any more than emotional crises can all be attributed to pathology.

Maria Daraki, in her book *Dionysos*, raises this paradox of a God whose cult grows in tandem with what it later opposes, a God who is heterodoxy within orthodoxy.[17] But if that seems like an untenable contradiction, perhaps it's from the angle of monotheism that any heterodoxy within an orthodoxy is seen as contradictory. The same impulse that denies that our societies regularly and normally produce revolutionaries and radicals of all kinds also refuses to admit that the liveliest and deepest relationships contain conflict. Christian monotheism has tried to eliminate Dionysos with such fierceness that we have become defensive about any sort of Dionysian destructiveness. So to be destructive, we need the fiction that we destroy to redress a wrong.

Dionysos remains a disturbing figure for any orthodoxy. He's the Other, the different one, the marginal one. Robin Lane Fox, comparing Christians and Pagans, notes that in monotheism there is conflict between orthodoxy (from *ortho* = right and *doxa* = opinion) and heterodoxy (from *hetero* = other); so Christians distinguish between those who think "right" and those who think "other," differently.[18] This contrast between rightness and divergence gives the impression that if you don't think like the orthodoxy you think wrongly. But to a pagan mentality, the more natural contrast is not between "thinking right" (orthodoxy) and "thinking differently" (heterodoxy), but between "thinking differently" (heterodoxy) and "thinking similarly," which is translated by homodoxy. Paganism does not react to differences with the same distress as monotheism does because it is based on plurality. This doesn't mean that the pagan attitude eliminates conflict, competition or combat. Opposition stemming from otherness remains, and the quarrels over territory between the Gods and Goddesses are witness to these tensions, but difference is rarely felt as an aberration. From the monotheistic point of view a Dionysos who disagrees, who represents the Other, is experienced not as an opponent to fight or discuss with, but as a deviance, a mistake, perhaps a monstrosity.

Michel Foucault has described eloquently how we eliminate differences and normalize the social order by shutting out, denying and pushing out of sight the lunatics, the sick, the retarded, and even the elderly, when the public standard only values youth,

intelligence, health and handsomeness.[19] The philosophical feminism of Simone de Beauvoir explores how women, once defined
as "The Other Sex," are then treated as inferior and incomprehen-
sible because of that Otherness.[20] She pleads for the need for
woman to rethink, from a philosophical point of view, the whole
question of differences. From another and more recent perspective, Luce Irigaray argues that the otherness of women has been
not only repressed by patriarchal culture but—even more important and alienating—this otherness has been defined by men, so
that we need to feel our own "otherness" and even have our own
language to define it.[21]

We need feminism because women are still deviations from masculine orthodoxy. In this, the truly pagan Dionysos can be an ally.
He is the one who shatters house walls and institutional walls,
who excites women and makes them want to run out into the wild,
who offers the exuberance of wine and drugs. Dionysos can be a
guide into the world of difference, but then one must expect that
he will threaten orthodoxies, both collective and personal.

The Favorite God of Woman

> This stranger they tell me has also come to town,
> this trickster magician from the Land of Lydia,
> this curly-haired goldilocks who perfumes his hair,
> who goes around with a sexy look in his eye,
> who gets together with girls, daytime and nighttime,
> proposing some secret pleasures to them,
> well if I ever get him inside,
> I'll put a stop to his wand-banging, I'll stop his hair
> from tossing, why I'll cut his head right off his neck,
> he's the one who says Dionysus is a god,
> he's the one who says he was sewn up in Zeus' thigh,
> when actually he and his mother both burned up
> in the flames of lightning, when she lied about Zeus loving her.
>
> Euripides, *The Bacchae*

In ancient times the "oak" Goddess reigned at Thebes, and every
year in July her priestesses, so the legend goes, sacrificed her king-
companion, cutting him into pieces and eating him. Robert Graves
offers the hypothesis that Dionysos's arrival in the myth marks the
end of the reign of the Goddess whose priestess, Semele, is struck

down by Zeus's power as she gives birth.[22] Priestess Semele is then replaced by a priest, and the Goddess by a God, Semele's son Dionysos.

In the classical period in Athens, there was still a yearly festival in honor of Semele—the "Lenaea"—where women evoked her old sovereignty through their dances. Under a shower of flower petals, a priest enjoined Semele to emerge from the navel of a belly-shaped altar and rejoin Dionysos, the spirit of spring. Dionysos, represented by an ox, was sacrificed, recalling the old custom of sacrificing the consort of the Great Goddess. The ox was cut up into nine parts, of which one was burned and the others eaten raw. Nine moon priestesses took part in the ritual.

By virtue of being Semele's son, Dionysos is presented as having kept a filial tie with this ancient feminine power. The "wild women" who often appear in association with him are described as wet-nurses, women who suckle their young and thereby have a privileged connection with animal nature. The fact that anthropologists attribute the domestication of animals to women who suckled the young of animals reinforces the image of these wild women who, like Dionysos, cross over the frontier between animal life and human life. Women who have given birth and nursed a baby know how sensitivity to animal life increases with pregnancy and childbirth, as if giving birth brings about the vivid consciousness of being a mammal. A young mother will not allow any young to be attacked, whether baby animals or baby humans, for her intimate connection with her own body as female mammal has made her cross over the psychological boundary from one kingdom to the other. A generosity flows with a mother's milk that can extend to everything that suckles, human or beast. The tale of Romulus and Remus nursed by a she-wolf and the tale of Tarzan indicate our belief in a similar generosity coming from the animal female. She too will suckle the abandoned human baby along with her own—or so we like to believe.[23]

It is well-known in animal psychology that there's nothing more ferocious than a female defending her young. Women retain something of this, and new mothers as well as their partners are sometimes troubled to discover to what extent a very timid woman can be transformed, the day after giving birth, into a brave, relentless, and violent female who will protect the baby, whatever the cost. A man who cannot understand this transformation needs

Dionysos to change his perceptions: he needs to experience human life as animal life. Since the way for him cannot be through giving birth, he needs the Dionysian Satyr, half man and half animal. Only then can he transpose the feminine experience of "feeling like an animal" that comes with giving birth and nursing a baby. This feeling is the perfect initiation for the Dionysian experience.

Euripides presents Dionysos as having the audacity to continue the teachings which were formerly lavished on women in the temple of their Goddesses. He sanctions the violence of the untamed mothers, and he encourages all women to drink wine and to develop a taste for Aphrodisian pleasures:

> It just so happens that while I'm out of town
> I hear about some new trouble in this city,
> how our women are leaving home
> pretending they're Bacchae or something, jumping in and out
> of the hill trees, dancing, all for this Dionysus god,
> who's the latest, whoever he is,
> and right in the middle of all this ruckus are their wine jugs,
> and each one sneaking off into a corner
> where she takes care of some man's lust
> on the excuse that they're maenad priestesses no less,
> while it's really Aphrodite they take care of before Bacchus, so that
> I've arrested some of them, and my deputies have them handcuffed
> for safe keeping in the prison,
> and those who got away I'll hunt down out of the hills,
> those like Ino, and even Agave, who's my mother through Echion,
> and Actaeon's mother too, Autonoë,
> all of whom I'll fit into iron nets
> and stop this Bacchic trouble-making right away. . . . [24]

According to legend, Dionysos was raised secretly in the forest, dressed like a girl to hide him from Hera. At the Dionysia both men and women dressed in a way that the Greeks considered effeminate. Dionysos has been sculpted with long curly hair, gentle, almost weak features, thick sensual lips and the look of a greedy child. True to his childlike nature he is both gentle and wild, cuddly and violent, brutish and witty, perverse and innocent, generous and demanding. Like a baby he is androgynous, feminine as much as masculine. Unlike Apollo, Dionysos isn't in a hurry to leave the world of women and doesn't show much haste to become a hero, being more comfortable in the role of women's darling. He lives surrounded by his nursemaids until late adolescence, and in some versions of the myth they went along with him as part of his cortege when he went off in search of his divinity!

The Dionysian man has to have his women around to take care of him, body and soul, to give him attention, lots of attention, to cuddle him, to excite him. He needs a woman to be wild, intense and sexy, but at the same time motherly, a generous mammalian animal giving the milk of compassion. He can be at times an ally, an accomplice in the woman's desire to escape the domestic routine, but at the same time he acts as a capricious child, demanding attention: "Where is my wife, my lover, my nanny, my nurse? I want my milk, my wine, my massage!"

This enjoyment of the company of women often puts him in conflict with the values personified by Zeus and Apollo. As the Greek aristocracy made these two their predominant divinities, Dionysos, honored by peasants, women, and slaves, was considered "vulgar." Platonic love was a move away from Dionysos and away from Aphrodite. The philosophical elite favored Eros over the heterosexual vigor of the Dionysias, and women were excluded from the celebration. "Whenever an intoxicating beverage is served women at a party/ it's the end of any good clean fun!" says Pentheus.[25] This was also the opinion of Plato and Aristotle and of those who later transformed Dionysos into a Christian Devil. All extreme rationalists are Pentheuses. To this day they try to lock up the God, opposing all of his manifold manifestations. Their rhetoric goes something like this:

> Get out of here—lock him up in the horse barn
> so that he can only see darkness and gloom—
> dance in *there*, and as for these ladies you've brought here,
> your co-workers in crime, I'll sell them for slaves
> or use them for laborers at my looms,
> but I'll stop their thumbs from strumming on drums![26]

Dionysos and Today's Eco-Feminism

A parallel can be drawn between the sexual repression of the Maenads at the end of Paganism, the repression of witches by the sexually demented Inquisitors in the Middle Ages, and the repression of feminine sexuality in the nineteenth century by puritanism, which classified as hysteria every kind of feminine rebellion of a sexual nature. There is also a certain aspect of "cock-teasing" in the Maenad that the Inquisitors tried to punish in every woman. The Maenad is always depicted with Satyrs, whose erections seem to try to get at her. She evokes the erection but will be caught only if she wishes. Some Maenads even wrap a snake around their bodies to protect them from the Satyrs but nevertheless tease them, dancing and running around them. The Maenad runs the sexual game.

The feminist Dionysia that we knew at the beginning of the 1960s were both an explosion of repressed feminine sexuality and an uprising of the maenadic anger, the two being connected. Women emerged from the dullness of depression into a frenzied Bacchanalia. Although the Dionysian men were happy to find wild sexual partners, others (the Pentheuses) were not only left out of the party, but psychologically and socially "torn to pieces" by the Maenads, whose name also means "women afflicted with rage," angry women whose rebellion could no longer be contained.

Jung has made of Dionysos the archetype who frees us from the tyranny of the ego, and archetypal psychology further describes Dionysos as a path of freedom for our inner oppressed woman.[27] Her liberation cannot be the result of an intentional, calculated, heroic process; it comes when the inner Maenad finally is let out, free to feel whatever she feels, including vulnerability as well as strength, distress as well as potency. The special gift of Dionysos is that bursting energy that breaks through the tyranny of the ego which will allow only one kind of feeling, that breaks through the internalization of Pentheus's rules and Platonic devaluation of the feminine.

Traditional psychoanalysis has disparaged and opposed everything in our consciousness that relates to vulnerability, weakness, and inferiority, because of their association with the feminine. To some extent, feminism itself has been caught in that trap, trying to break the association of femininity and weakness. Seeing through the myth of analysis, James Hillman shows how the end of a traditional analysis is the moment when the patient finally eradicates weak, passive, suffering inner femininity from his personality. Hillman demonstrates how the myth of psychoanalysis is Apollonian, at war with any feeling of feminine inferiority which must be rooted out in order for one to be cured—that is, to be virile as Apollo would define it.

Psychoanalysis somehow has convinced us that it must "make a man" of our weak, irrational, hysteric inner woman, because neither weakness, nor maenadism, nor receptivity, nor femininity is valued as part of the human experience. Wasn't the first act of psychoanalysis to replace Dionysos, God of women, with a diagnosis of hysteria? A radical Dionysian change of direction in the basic premises of psychotherapy would set the goal of analysis as the return of Dionysos, of the Maenads and of the many Goddesses to consciousness.

Dionysos is called "Zoe": biological life, animal life. There is an element in him—as in Demeter, Hestia, and Artemis—that is a celebration, a passivity of nature in *sui generis*, a "doing very little" that has been denigrated as feminine. There must be a Dionysian ecology, not just a scientific one of Apollo or an Artemisian one. But this receptive quality of Dionysos will need some feminist rhetoric before it's available to our consciousness. Celebrating and deepening our intimacy with animal life, a Dionysian ecology is a profound receptivity to animals that is not just a "study in interspecies communication" but its enjoyment; instead of taking note, one seeks a deep instinctive intimacy with the animal. The surest way to that kind of relationship is, paradoxically, to do very little, to simply release our own animal, to be delighted, entranced by the presence of the animal in front of us, to let it come to us. Dian Fossey, the most famous specialist on gorillas, is a good example of what a Dionysian ecology might achieve. She almost became "one of them," loved them so much it cost her her life. She did not fight for the gorilla out of heroism, but out of passionate love for that form of animal life. Her method was Dionysian, and her uncompromising attitude was Artemisian, although she added to it the discipline of a trained scientist.

Domestic Tyrants

If it's true that Dionysos is an ally of all oppressed femininity, a liberator opposed to inquisitors of all kinds, we must remember that a liberator usually doubles as a tyrant, which brings up some problematic aspects of the Dionysian masculine personality in relationship to women. The Dionysian man has a sensual, expansive, ardent quality that women appreciate in a lover. He is at ease in their world since he himself possesses so many qualities (and weaknesses) that are labeled "feminine." He seems to enjoy life through his very weaknesses: "I am mad," "I belong to nature and to woman," "I go with the flow," "I get drunk and that's good." But there is also a problematic side to this soft, flabby, love-needy personality. One thinks of the Mediterranean, psychopathic, unscrupulous loverboy, like a male prostitute, a seducer of women (out of the house, out of the normal life of chores and duty). In other words, we need to see the disgusting aspect of the God, for he is also a serpent, a loosener—all characteristics emphasized by most Apollonic scholars studying Dionysos. There is a hysterical tyrant in him, which we should not whitewash.

We need to remember his physical appearance: soft belly, plumpness, long hair and fair skin (*The Bacchae*). These are also metaphors, psychological qualities that make him soft and wild at once, ardent lover and soft child, powerful animal and cuddly baby. One thinks of Presley, Brando and all those free, wild, sexy, mad loverboys who attract women. He can be full of enthusiasm, sparkling with excitement; his energy wakes people up, draws them into dancing and celebrating, into the emotion of the moment. When he's not around, the world seems dull. At other times he is the humid night, the silent, patient, moist darkness of biological development.

Up to a point it's easy to see why the Dionysian personality attracts women: they want to be part of the Bacchanalia and to protect the childlike vitality of their wild lover. But Dionysian men can show the most hysterical woman a thing or two about throwing dishes around, slamming doors, threatening suicide or retaliation, tearing their clothes, shouting, crying, kicking and punching. Their childlike qualities can engender tyrannical, love-greedy relationships that exhaust women. Men who display moderation and rationality in their professional lives can exhibit such domestic tyranny; they cannot tolerate not having a woman to look after them and mother them! Dionysos the Liberator has become Dionysos the Tyrant.

As a feminist, I have often wondered why there's never a lack of women to nurse the souls of these dark Dionysian men, to feed and support them, to be to them as Cybele, healer and teacher, or as Thetis who gives Dionysos shelter, or as the Maenads who form his fan-club. What nerve in women do they touch? If I look into my own experience, I would risk the idea that the Dionysian man steals the place of the ravenous baby whose pummeling of our nipples is acceptable because he's hungry, right this minute, he's so hungry. We're attached to an infant through his very need for us. We're captivated by the amazing process whereby the more the baby draws milk the more it flows. The more the child is ravenous, the more the mother gives. We become identified with Demeter–Cybele, divine Mother, horn of plenty, the infinitely generous Great Mother, while he identifies with the God, son-lover of the Goddess.

As we yield to the desires of a child, so we yield to the desires of the Dionysian man: they're so intense and seem so essential to his nature. The man receives by the very need he has to be taken care of, and the woman is lured into colluding with this scenario of substitution. I see no problem as long as the substitution is playful or as long as both partners feel empowered in some reciprocal way: I the cornucopia and you the ever demanding child-lover. There can be pleasure on both sides. But a problem usually develops if (a) the man has a propensity to mega-tantrums and tyrannical whims, or (b) if there are real children around and the possessive partner desires to dislodge them in order to have all the attention, or (c) the woman becomes so exhausted that she cannot go on identifying with the ever-generous Mother-Goddess. As her Cybele–Demeter–Thetis complex takes its toll on her energy, the cornucopia is emptied.

What is the psycho-mythological background for that lure? Some women will tell you they see the child in the adult man when he attacks them with all the strength of a man's physique. Women victims of conjugal violence often describe their mates as children having a tantrum, as if there were no difference between the kick of a frustrated two-year-old and the blow that breaks their ribs.

Almost all admit they are easily cajoled by the tears of a repentant husband, the confessed dependency: "don't leave me, I can't get along without you, I won't do it again," etc., followed by intense love-making or dramatic promises. They don't realize they're forgiving adult violence as if it were done by a child. The more a woman acquiesces in the substitution, the more she gives and forgives. Of course, one can see that the man touches the maternal nerve. But which Mother image is behind her? In the Dionysian myth, the Mother-figures are powerful Goddesses. They will not be abused even by an ultra-demanding Dionysos.

These abused women are trapped in a confusion between the Christian Mater Dolorosa, the unassertive sacrificial mother, and the Pagan Demeter who offers bread and milk to humanity but keeps her Goddess's power and the aggressiveness that goes with it. When a man's voraciousness exhausts a mother's resources and there's no longer enough time, enough love, enough money, enough space, or even enough happiness essential to the survival of the children, it's time to meditate on Demeter, who refuses to nourish humanity when something wrong happens in the relationship. Goddess Demeter does not tolerate being deprived of her child or that her child be deprived of her. The myth wisely associates hungry Dionysos with Demeter's good sense. Whatever the needs of the son-lover and however chaotic the orgy, the Mother Goddess doesn't allow the nest to be burned or her resources to be exhausted. A needy Dionysian man needs a strong Demeterian mothering. The weak, thin, and much too young Virgin-Mother-Mary is no match for this ravenous Rabelaisian child.

Women victims of conjugal violence usually wake up when they realize the wrong being done to their children, not because their own suffering has peaked. It is then that they break the identification with the sacrificial Mother who has no desires, no intensity, no violence of her own and stand up to the man who threatens their children. The image of a saddened Demeter separated from her daughter has been likened by Hellenists to a Pagan Mater Dolorosa. There is in fact a statue of Demeter in mourning, a marble discovered at Cnide, that expresses well her woman's pain at the loss of her child. But unlike the Christian Mater Dolorosa, Demeter finds tears are not the only answer: she is angry and refuses to exchange good for evil, food for pain. Here is one of the fundamental differences between Christianity and Paganism: the Mother-Goddess threatens God-the-Father-Zeus, who allowed the abduction, with letting humanity die of hunger. As long as her daughter is not returned to her, nothing will germinate and she will not nourish humankind. She goes on strike, and she won't give an inch. That, to my eyes, is a convincing Mother-Goddess. What is a mother worth if she won't stand up for her child? Dionysos can be a tyrant, Zeus can be a tyrant (although in a different mode), and sometimes there is no hope for change. The right relationship to that problem might be to find in ourselves the Demeterian attitude.

Mary, on the other hand, shows the psychology of a battered woman: here is her son, nailed to a cross, humiliated, tortured to death, and she will have no aggressiveness, only tears and lamentations! Her only and famous line, the line we were given as the model of feminine receptivity, gives a clue to her character: *"I am the handmaid of the Lord, let what you have said be done to me."*[28] No mature woman would have such a torpid reaction. I believe that is why we have had, for centuries, pietàs that show Mary with the face of a young girl and never like the woman she must have been when her son reached thirty-three years of age! Her helplessness, if not cowardice, was glorified as the virtue of resignation.

But who, really, would like to be the son of a woman so helpless she stands by a creed that asks for her son to be sacrificed? This is one consequence of sexist religions without Mother-Goddesses: the sons, as well as the daughters, are sacrificed to the glory or sadism of the father. To Pagan eyes, a Goddess who wouldn't have the guts to defend her child wouldn't deserve to be presented as a Mother figure. The Pagan morality (as the contemporary feminist morality) assumes that one returns good for good: Demeter rewarded King Keleos and the Eleusinians for their hospitality. But unlike the Christian ethic, the Pagan ethic (as the contemporary feminist ethic) returns evil for evil. There can be no ambiguity on that point on the part of Demeter: no daughter, no food. To return good for evil is to be Christian. For a woman the conjunction between Christian morality and political powerlessness means she ends up in the position of the archetypal Christian Mother: she must accept, without raising her voice, the sacrifice of her child.

One may further ask: "But who is torturing the Son?" And the answer sounds frightening: it is the Father! The only star figure that Christianity presents to women is a mother who hasn't enough strength to stop the father from sacrificing, from torturing the child in order to show his power and his glory as All-Powerful-Father-God.

Mary certainly has spiritual qualities of her own that I do not wish to depreciate. One can look at her as the Sophia, a figure of wisdom and compassion, or as the proof of a Pagan underground resistance to an all-male religion. There is no unique way to consider an archetype. But she is definitely not an appropriate role model as the submissive mother who feels the father has a "right" to inflict violence on the children, which is after all the truth of the matter in extremely patriarchal societies. The women's unconscious reverence for the Father figure of traditional religion threatens the family whenever there is no counter-image of a strong Mother who could say "No!" As persons, but also as mothers, they need to unlearn the attitude of Mary and move toward Demeter, the assertively and—if need be—aggressively protective Goddess of the mother–child relationship. Demeter will not have the child devour the mother nor the lover drink the milk meant for the baby.

Who Is Ariadne, Dionysos's Wife?

The myth presents Ariadne as a daughter of Minos, King of Crete, and Pasiphae, who, having coupled with a gigantic bull, gave birth to the Minotaur. The monster, half-brother to Ariadne, is locked up in a labyrinth built by Daedalus, an Athenian architect who had sought refuge at the court of Minos. Every nine years, King Minos claims a tribute of seven girls and seven boys from Athenian families. These young people are devoured by the Minotaur or lose their way and die in the labyrinth. The young hero Theseus arrives one day on the same boat as the young Athenians who are going to be sacrificed. Ariadne meets Theseus and, finding him attractive, cooks up a plan to help him do away with the Minotaur. She offers to help him get out of the labyrinth after killing the monster, in exchange for a promise that he will marry her and take her with him to Athens. Ariadne solicits advice from Daedalus, and they work out the idea of giving Theseus a ball of thread to unwind as he disappears into the labyrinth, thus assuring a way out.

When Theseus emerges victorious from the maze, Ariadne runs away with him as planned. But she never reaches Athens. During a stopover on the isle of Naxos, she falls asleep on the bank and wakes up to find Theseus's boat pulling away, leaving her alone on the shore. At this moment Dionysos appears, approaching her in a chariot drawn by black panthers, and takes her off to Olympus. The young God marries her and gives her as a wedding present a crown made by Hephaestos that in time will become a constellation of stars. Dionysos will be faithful to Ariadne, the only God to be so faithful to his wife.

The explanation for Theseus's abandoning Ariadne varies according to different versions of the legend. One says that he loves another woman, Aegle. In another he "forgets" her, obeying Dionysos who has already fallen in love with Ariadne. Or else it's Athena or even Hermes who persuades Theseus to abandon her, because his (or her) destiny is elsewhere. There's also a version in which the ship is blown by a storm to Cyprus. Ariadne, already pregnant and seasick, disembarks to get some sleep. Theseus goes back on board to look after the ship, but a gust of wind carries it out to sea and he can't return for her. The women on the island take care of Ariadne and bring her letters they write themselves pretending Theseus sent them. Ariadne dies giving birth. When Theseus returns for the child, he establishes a ritual in her honor. On the way home Theseus stops off at Delos where he consecrates a statue of Aphrodite Ariadne had given him. On that occasion he performs, along with the young people he has saved from being sacrificed, a complicated dance in which he turns around and around, retracing his steps to represent the complexity of the labyrinth.

All versions speak to the imagination, but the durable core of the legend says simply that Ariadne goes to sleep and awakes as the boat pulls away; at that moment Dionysos appears and carries her off to Olympus. We don't really know why Ariadne finds herself alone on the shore. All mythological stories contain mysteries, imprecisions—"holes" in the narration which raise questions. But it's in this very imprecision—which, dream-like, doesn't necessarily make connections between events—that a trigger for our imagination is sometimes found. The meaning of a myth has to be renewed over and over and always requires filling in the missing places. The Greeks ventured to complete a narration in terms of the consciousness of each age, thus keeping their mythology alive, while ours is fixed in dogma.

While writing this chapter on Dionysos, whose first draft dates back ten years, I've questioned myself regularly about this scene of abandonment, not finding a satisfactory interpretation. To tell the truth, this story burned me up. Ariadne looked like the archetypal Dupe, the Deserted Woman, the Woman Wronged. I saw her as the first in a long line of women who participate in the success of the hero-husband only to find themselves at some later point alone, deprived of their share of the benefits. Ariadne helps Theseus get his M.D. or Ph.D. by doing secretarial work, and when his career is in full swing, he asks for a divorce and leaves her with the kids, without a job, or a car, or money, on the shore of some desolate suburban island. Most of all, I didn't like the fact that she is stuck there on the beach, *waiting for another prince*, until the great Dionysos turns up beside her. Once again, this time with Dionysos instead of Theseus, she seems the accessory to someone else's fame; she, the beautiful Ariadne, looks like a trophy for Dionysos at the end of his voyage of conquest. He needs her to make a glorious entry into Olympus in his luxurious carriage drawn by two black panthers. Ariadne the archetypal groupie?

And to say one more nasty thing about her: she gets herself into this new relationship *while the ship of her rejecting lover is still in sight*, as if she couldn't live a minute without another love affair. This poor second start would make her a woman who owes everything to the person rescuing her from depression and abandonment. The Ariadne myth seemed so demoralizing and so reactionary that I wasn't able to enjoy it as I did most other myths. I wanted to see it as worn-out, now that feminism has taught us to recognize a fool's bargain when we see one and to be less dependent on a Prince Charming.

But if a myth could be outmoded it wouldn't be a myth any longer. It would no longer trigger the imaginative process, nor even the irritation that is often a sign that the myth needs to be reinterpreted. When we say a myth is "dead," we mean a certain interpretation is used up, defunct, but the myth itself has more than one life. Since there's no dogma for the interpretation of myths, they are there to be reinterpreted continually, just as we keep reinterpreting the events in our lives that have touched us. Myth in this sense resembles the facts of a biography; it gives genealogies and events. It says, for instance, Ariadne falls asleep on the beach, and when she wakes up Theseus's ship is pulling away. Later she takes Dionysos as spouse and ascends with him to heaven. But as in our own biography, interpreted differently each time we tell our life-story although it is always based on the same facts, no interpretation of a myth can be definitive. In this case the fact is that, when Ariadne wakes up, the ship is setting sail. But what sort of fiction will one weave around that fact? One can say Ariadne misses the boat, or that she gets off that particular boat, or that she is abandoned. Same fact, but a different consciousness of it.

I lost my annoyance for Ariadne's story first by reading and re-reading the principal version of the myth; there I felt that one can interpret the facts in such a way that Ariadne is not at all a passive woman, but quite a fascinating heroine. She is the one who chooses Theseus, not the other way around. It is said she finds him attractive and falls in love with him, but it's also stated that she sees in him a way to escape the house of her father, King Minos. In exchange for her help she makes Theseus promise to take her far away, to Athens. She therefore knows what she wants, and as soon as she sees in him a chance to leave home she acts. She has a taste for rebellion (rebellion against the Minotaur, against her father's authority). Theseus can thus be seen as instrumental in her destiny instead of the reverse, that she is instrumental in his fate.

She has a sense of initiative and planning which allows her to realize that it isn't enough for brave Theseus to kill the Minotaur: he also has to get out of the labyrinth. Heroes, especially typically masculine ones like Theseus, are not always foresighted—and he least of all. He's so forgetful he causes his father's suicide through negligence. (When he returns to Athens and fails to change the black sails, sign of defeat, to white sails indicating victory, his father kills himself in despair.) But Ariadne, like most heroines, has a gifted intelligence and strategic sense. She prepares carefully for Theseus's mission and consults the right person, Daedalus. Together they invent the ruse of Ariadne's ball of thread, which is so simple and so inspired that ever since it has symbolized an idea, a feeling, a person or anything that serves as a key or main clew to follow to reorient oneself in a complex, confused environment.

We remember Ariadne and her thread every time we find ourselves in an intellectual maze, or an inextricable emotional muddle, or an imbroglio of relationships that we can't get out of. To be in a maze is to know there's a way out but not to be able to find the right path; we can't help going round in circles, feeling anguished. Theseus's type of courage, needed to kill the Minotaur, is no help in this context. It takes the genius of Ariadne, the crafty heroine, who anticipates, consults, talks it over, and comes up with a simple, creative idea that resolves the most incredibly confused situation. Her plan having met with success, as expected, the heroine sets sail with the hero. But she falls asleep on the beach at Naxos, and her destiny takes another turn. What gets into her to fall asleep at such a moment? How can a young heroine as smart as she is, as careful about details, let herself be so badly duped?

A myth can be examined from many vantage points: usually we look at it from beginning to end, as a normal story goes. But we can also find meaning by looking first at the end of Ariadne's story. Then we see that, in order to escape her future with Theseus and make contact with Dionysos, she has to fall asleep and miss the boat. It is as if Ariadne always knew that life as Theseus's wife is not enough for her; she sleeps as a means to avoid one man and wait for the other.

When I think of all the times in my life I've slept through my resistance to something, or I've escaped into sleep so that people would leave me alone, or I've literalized soporific situations by falling asleep in them, or I've stayed in a kind of semi-consciousness until a situation became openly dramatic, I like to think of Ariadne's sleep as a semi-conscious choice. It is said that Ariadne goes to sleep and her destiny changes. It may be that Ariadne goes to sleep so that her destiny may change, so that Theseus can go away. She chooses, even if semi-consciously, not to embark with Theseus because she wants someone else—Dionysos.

Ariadne is a heroine, and heroines are often attracted to antiheroes. Dionysos is divine but not so heroic. He seems to be saying: "I need someone to look after me; I want pleasure; I wear my hair long; I wear a dress; I belong to the night, to nature, to celebration, to emotion, to women. I want love, not war." By contrast Theseus is a typical mortal hero, returning to Athens to continue his hero's career, more interested in politics than in love. Ariadne's association with Theseus is a marriage that doesn't work: she dozes off, lets life go by. Maybe she does not know exactly toward what other shores she may want to drift; all she knows is what she doesn't want. Like many other divorcées, one morning there she is, alone on the beach ready for the next step in her destiny.

When Dionysos arrives, Ariadne recognizes him as the one she has been waiting for: a warm-hearted, intense God is the right companion for this intelligent planner of a woman. And he offers to "take her to heaven," whatever meaning one chooses to give that expression. He also gives her a wedding present, whereas with Theseus she had to help him out first so that he would take her with him. To go to Olympus is certainly more appealing than to take her place in the gynaeceum of the hero's house, and this time she sets off with Dionysos without falling asleep. With a spouse like Dionysos, Ariadne's talents will not likely be overlooked. Dionysos lives in a dense maze of emotions, a labyrinth of sensations; she is the thread.

So, in the end, Ariadne does well to fall asleep so as not to get back on Theseus's ship. Whatever is said of her feelings on the beach, one must remember that heroines are never turned into crybabies by an unhappy love affair. The trial marriage to Theseus is not the final step. Rather, the pairing of intense Dionysos with the mistress of the labyrinth is the final goal. Each Dionysos needs his Ariadne; each Ariadne-type heroine needs her Dionysos to take her to heaven.

The Invention of Tragedy

In the preface to a book by Jean Pierre Vernant, Pierre Vidal-Naquet has this to say about the connection between Dionysos and tragedy:

> Nothing in the themes, in the texture of the works, in the unfolding of the spectacle is especially connected to Dionysos who is something of a loner within the Greek pantheon. They have tried to understand Greek tragedy by going back to its religious beginnings; they wanted to grasp its true meaning by uncovering the old

Dionysian core from which it supposedly emerged so as to reveal the secret of tragedy in all its purity. Risky business at the factual level, illusory and futile in terms of principle.[29]

Vidal-Naquet concludes: "Tragedy was, in the strongest sense of the term, an invention."[30] The power of tragedy, then, didn't come from some obscure past, more or less primitive and mystical, but from the originality of the invention. What was original about tragedy? And if tragedy was an invention of the fifth and sixth centuries B.C., the question Plutarch asked may well be repeated: "What did Dionysos have to do with tragedy?" Vernant and Vidal-Naquet suggest that Dionysos is connected with what was new about tragedy, that is, a work of art produced out of pure artifice. For the first time the Greek audience was listening to dialogues invented from a playwright's imagination. For the first time the playwright was freed from having to recite the exploits of heroes who presumably "really" existed, from passing on the epic, from doing oral history. He could imagine a whole play and dramatize inner conflicts "as if" they were real.

Classical tragedy, the first "fictional" work, started with the first performance under Pisistratus in 534 B.C. Its great success coincided with the development of a new consciousness. It is as if the Greeks learned, through the artist, about individual consciousness, the "I" who deliberates, who is not the plaything of the Gods and destiny anymore. Even though fictional, the works of tragedy actually changed the existing mentality, and this change, the new consciousness, is classical tragedy's most lasting accomplishment. As actors dialogued with themselves and with each other and for the first time dared to decide their own personal destinies, Homeric consciousness evolved toward modern individualistic consciousness.

We must not limit the Dionysian perspective to the tragic alone, in spite of this old connection between Dionysos and tragedy, for it's through its storytelling aspect, rather than its catastrophic events, that tragedy resembles Dionysos. Our tendency to restrict Dionysos to suffering and tragic persecution comes from our heroic mentality which wants to make him the victim of his exalted emotions. Heroic mentality goes after each situation as if to root out every problem, every drama, all the tension that springs from conflict. But within the Dionysian perspective things are not experienced that way: "Dionysian consciousness understands the conflicts in our stories through dramatic tensions and not through conceptual opposites; we are composed of agonies not polarities."[31] One has to let go of the heroic posture to understand Dionysos, to stop analyzing contradictions, complexes, and problems with the idea of resolving and eventually eliminating them. The Dionysian impulse is not to stand back, analyze, and take control of the situation but to jump into the action and play a part in a scenario full of developments and new understandings about life itself. Writers of fiction are well aware that you can't produce interesting work if the main character only submits to the will of others and doesn't stand up for himself. According to John Gardner, author and professor, who has led many workshops on writing fiction, the most common failing of amateur novelists is to present a character to whom things happen instead of one who controls his own destiny.[32] A character to whom things happen is a Homeric character, not a fictional one.

The same failing, transferred to the psychological level, usually leads us into therapy: we become fed up with submitting to the unconscious, with watching our dreams every night as a passive spectator. In our own life-scripts we commit the error of the amateur writer: being a passive character, seated in the audience instead of going on stage. That's what being deprived of Dionysos means, for he's the God of dramatic imagination. Therapy begins when we enter into the drama, and it progresses as a rewriting of the life-script—this time correcting the beginner's mistakes. It's not only feelings that are subject to revisioning but the story itself within which they are experienced. James Hillman develops this theme by playing on the double meaning of the title *Healing Fiction* understood as "to heal fiction" and "fiction that heals."[33] He shows how the fiction we create around the events of our lives can also undergo revision, because it's not only the person who is sick but the stories the person tells himself to make sense of his experiences. There's more than one way to tell our story, and some versions can make us sick. The stories then need to be treated, edited. Therapy is a course in rewriting the scenario we live by. We edit, correct, modify our part and restore our sense of participation as the principal character of that particular drama.

Playing Roles, Wearing Masks

> The child who dresses up as a king, the prince who
> disguises himself as a pauper, the blacksmith who
> likes to wear women's dresses and the seamstress
> who puts on a soldier's uniform, the timid person
> who when masked becomes bold, the hunchback
> roaring from inside a tiger's head—all these are in
> some way paying homage to Dionysos for a day,
> for an hour, and thereby freeing themselves of
> secret desires and buried regrets.
>   Maurice Druon, *Les Mémoires de Zeus*

Dionysos, God of carnivals and masquerades and patron saint of actors, is also the masked God or the God of masks. Children, women and ordinary people have always loved disguises and carnivals. Since those in power utilize the trappings of masquerade (i.e., judges' robes, military uniforms, the silks and tiaras of the Church, medals and thrones, etc.), those left out claim for themselves the right to become multiple, to become impressive, magnificent, something other than what they are. A society that no longer puts on carnivals and costumed events loses an important psychological resource and impoverishes the collective imagination.

And there's more. The expression "to wear a mask" also means "to play a role." It's from this perspective of a masked God, a God who loves to play many roles, that we discover an ordinary, everyday Dionysos, in addition to the Dionysos of great occasions, celebrations and stage sets. This day-to-day Dionysos is as important as the other, the one I have been writing about so far, for he is the inspiration for the personal and social roles that life in society invites us to play.

The ideas that follow may seem far from the figure of the God of the Bacchanals, but I like to think this is because our interpretation of his myth so far has left out a part that I would like to explore. Maybe it is the social psychologist in me that is coming to the surface again, eager to see in his myth a possibility for the renewal of the role theory, so central to my discipline.

But first, let's begin with an anecdote to illustrate how role and mask are not necessarily instruments of disguise. One of my colleagues is a psychologist with a somewhat unusual practice. She works in partnership with doctors who refer spouses of patients who are terminally ill or who have chronic afflictions. She does not see the patient, only the spouse. After five years of practice, she has found that those spouses who have had to take care of young children, on top of the burden of the sick husband or wife, are somehow better off. Even if this situation means more work, fatigue, and heavy responsibilities, the spouses are less depressed and recover more quickly from their companions' deaths than do the others. Curious about this finding, she asked them why they are in better shape than those with fewer responsibilities and more free time.

Each in his or her own way told her that the day-to-day closeness with small children forced one to act cheerfully, to hide distress and grief, to play cool even when the feeling inside was despair. An even worse situation might develop—or get completely nightmarish—if the children were to catch the anxieties of the adult. Inasmuch as the self-possessed, serene, friendly parent who puts the children to bed, who cooks and serves meals, who gives a bath or tells a bedtime story is a cheerful role, the adult finds in these moments an escape from the sad and often devastating situation.

The parent who pretends that everything is peaceful, in spite of the pain and turmoil he may be experiencing, is playing with the child who, in turn, guides him and feeds him lines. The parent and the child have an unconscious contract: they make believe that 'everything is going well.' It would be absurd to ask them if they're being truthful, just as it is foolish to question whether a child is being truthful when he's playing. It is honest truth and honest play. They are playing and it's doing them both a lot of good. Games only become false when we take them literally, when we call them 'reality'—that is, when we want to stop playing and get serious.

Their experience is not so far from ours, with or without children, with or without a sick spouse. Who hasn't been in a desperate emotional situation while at the same time being forced to maintain a cheerful mask? For example, to be in a position where you have to show professional attitudes of enthusiasm and receptivity, when you would rather show a grim mask, feels at first like an effort. But often the feeling that was being acted becomes ours, and we become one with the mask.

That is how I understand the popularity of such a simplistic psychological approach as "Positive Thinking." This approach is built around one fundamental prescription: to replace the negative roles and fantasies by positive ones. If I repeat to myself, "I am strong, I am strong" often enough, and if I act as if I were strong, then I may become strong. Apart from the fact that one cannot build a whole psychology exclusively on the positive side of a single inner experience, no more than on a single archetype, and apart from a certain simple-minded application of the method, one can see why this approach arouses interest. For those who wear the mask of boredom, timidity and inferiority, positive thinking can act as a training ground for a more relaxed or powerful role.

To act as if you were untroubled while feeling panicked might seem a lie. But this is because one assumes that there is one and only one genuine emotion and that any behavior that is not an expression of that one, deep, true emotion is deceptive. In a book called *The Presentation of Self in Everyday Life*, Irving Goffman defines sincerity as "trust in our own performance," while cynicism would be not to care about the audience and to mock those who believe in our performance.[34] These definitions of sincerity and cynicism are suited to a Dionysian point of view. The actor does not feel he is cheating about his identity because he knows, as we do, that he is playing a role, wearing a mask. If he is not cynical, in Goffman's sense, he puts all of himself into his role and tries to be for the audience the character he pretends to be. Meanwhile the actor is not bothered about whether he is being true to his 'real self.' He is truly an actor. As we all are.

Dionysos is not the God behind the mask. He is the mask.

In our psychological culture, the quest for the real and true Self conceals an anti-Dionysian fantasy and a typically monotheistic one. We do not easily recognize Dionysos, patron of actors, who invites us to play every role, tragic as well as comic, grotesque as well as solemn, with intensity, with spirit and brio. To know Dionysos, we must accept identification with the mask instead of searching for something behind it. That identification, intense as it may be, is temporary. As God of carnival, of the masquerade, he is concerned with the constant metamorphosis of identity and opposed to any fixed identification with a role. To be Dionysian, one needs not only to identify fully with the person, animal or divinity pictured by the mask but also to accept that this identification is never definitive and final. As soon as there is no more playing around, no more movement, we leave Dionysos for some other style (maybe Zeus, or Hestia, who does not like changes).

The Dionysos best known to mythologists and anthropologists is related to the Bacchanalia or to classical Greek tragedy, since the God had his shrine on the stage and his priest had a seat of honor in the theater. But one can ask: why is it that Dionysos is so often restricted to the classical form of theater, while other Gods and Goddesses were not restricted to their temples? What about the Maenads dancing in the mountains? We easily understand, for example, that Aphrodite is present whenever there is sexual attraction, and we can recognize her in timid, uncertain desire as well as in the most ecstatic or extravagant sexual experience. So why not acknowledge Dionysos wherever and whenever there is fantasy, dramatization, role-playing?

One cannot escape fantasy, even when one narrates only the real facts of one's life. Wherever there is a Narrator (and how could there not be?), there is no objective biography, no more than objective history, since any biography implies an archetypal perspective from which the events, the moods, the qualities that make up the story are selected. The same life-story can be told from my point of view as hero or from my point of view as victim. As we often see in therapy, a woman who, in front of her friends, tells her story as an ongoing feminist combat against machismo will be, in a different context, feeling and telling her story from the point of view of the submissive wife, the traditional mother, the faithful daughter. We have many stories, many biographies, because we are inhabited by many archetypal persons and are constantly editing our life-script. Walter Ong claims that there is a process he calls "fictionalization" not only in pre-literate, oral cultures, as is already well recognized, but in our literate culture as well. No writer, he argues, can write without fantasizing a public. Even the personal diary, which is not meant for any avowed audience, implies a certain stage-setting, since we fancy ourselves in the role of the Narrator.

Dionysos is usually presented as an extravagant, intemperate figure, which is certainly an important aspect of the archetype. But this keeps him within the boundaries of carnival-like occasions, or tragic and intense situations, and so excludes him from everyday life. And we lose the day-to-day Dionysos, the God of masks. To know him is not to unmask him, but to take a deeper look at the mask.

Already, in the fifties, Simone de Beauvoir did take a deeper look at the masks worn by men and women. She described in detail how a strong woman will put on a show of helplessness and end up believing it herself, how young girls deliberately lose in competitive games with boys, and how an adult woman is asked not to challenge the superiority of men's opinions and status. Together with the long line of feminist scholars who later wrote about gender roles, she understood that the feminine mask was designed for the convenience of the male audience, not to enhance women's performance. Feminism pointed out how cynical it inevitably becomes when a man and woman are forced to act in a play they despise, with masks with which they cannot identify. In such a context, we still need Dionysos's ferocity and chaos to destroy the old roles, to wreck the stage, to wipe out the scenario, to overthrow the directors and, most difficult of all, to overturn in ourselves the rigidity of old habits. We need to be reminded that we are role-playing, that nothing is fixed.

When roles feel like a yoke—binding, curbing and hampering us—they can be dropped occasionally, as in the Bacchanalia, or permanently, as in revolution and revolt. But the day-to-day Dionysos can also act more gently, precisely by helping us not to take play literally. For Jean Pierre Vernant, the French classicist, Dionysos shatters the positivist perspective, for which there is only one interpretation, one truth, one definite place for everything and everyone.[35] He defines Dionysos as the God who introduces us to the world of Otherness. To be able to play many roles we must have this built-in sense of the other.

Of course, one must find a balance between the pathology of the one who thinks he wears no mask and plays no games and the pathology of the one who cannot commit himself to long-term, substantial roles, feeling that every attitude is role-playing anyway, that nothing is real or worth being taken to heart. The first believes he plays no role, while in fact he plays only one and rigidly sticks to it, while the second is a poor actor, his performance inadequate from lack of rehearsals and botched staging. When we are faced with a bad performance, our weird feeling does not come from the fact that someone is wearing a mask but from the fact that the mask is worn awry. Psychologists will more readily see the pathology of the one who believes that everything is a game than the one who believes that he plays none. Let's not forget that psychology has often favored a definition of mental health with no room for play. Pierre Janet, for example, an early and influential theoretician of scientific psychology, described maturity as the choice of one's identity and the end of an open multi-directionality. The straitening and fixation of the ego was conceived as the final stage in the construction of the personality. Janet insisted on the negative side of role-playing, on tension and contradictions between roles, and the necessity of the unity of personality.

Humanistic psychology took the opposite direction inasmuch as it assumed the multiplicity of roles in everyday life. But still, the humanist's quest for the authentic Self can also be taken as anti-Dionysian, since the mask of Dionysos is not something behind which one hides, but rather the very image through which one connects to the archetype. The ascetic, who will never allow a little fun, a little drunkenness, who forbids excess and fears intensity, is not the only anti-Dionysian type. The fantasy that one day I will find my authentic self, the one behind the mask, behind the mirror, behind the roles, is also anti-Dionysian. The denial of Dionysos carries a dangerous separation between my True Self, on the one hand, which I define as good, deep and authentic, and, on the other hand, the social role, which doesn't depend on me, which is only a mask I'm obliged to wear to live in the world and which excuses me from questioning the sanctity of my deep self.

Carried to its extreme, such a refusal to identify with the mask leads to the type of person who could become a Nazi torturer while continuing to see himself as sensitive and refined because in his private life he listens to Mozart with emotion. He doesn't call into question his 'True Self,' since he's sensitive, he loves music, children and flowers. It's the other who wears a military uniform and behaves like a brute, but that one is only a mask, a mask that hides the True Sensitive Self. If one is truly Dionysian, there is no way to know who is behind the mask, since the mask itself is a divinity, and a divinity won't be treated like an accessory that one can hang in the closet. Carl Kerényi mentions that modern man seems to be obsessed with the idea that if we could put aside all masks we would be liberated and the original, good, primitive man would stand revealed.[36] But, again, this negative definition of the mask as something behind which one hides is just the opposite of the ancient concept of mask as a link between the person and the archetypal animal, ancestor, or divinity it embodied.

Our negative attitude toward someone we see as 'wearing a mask' is not a negative attitude toward the mask, but a refusal to let him play a certain role because of the power vested in that role. We do not agree, for example, that so and so has a right to adopt a paternal attitude toward us or to put on a face that implies superiority. We defend ourselves, not against masks, but against those we perceive as thieves, stealing powerful masks they have no right to wear. When the adolescent rebels against adult roles, we tend to see a fresh young soul cutting through the falseness of adult games and suffering from our lack of authenticity. There is some truth in that because adolescents can insight the falseness of certain attitudes. But it could also be that the adolescent is expressing his frustration because he has had to wait too long for an opportunity to play a consistent role. The roles offered him lack substance, variety, intensity. Adolescents complain by booing our performance as adults. Their anger resembles that of feminists discovering the insignificance, the loneliness and the contempt that go along with some women's roles. These women won't applaud the masculine hero for the same reasons that the young put down adults who monopolize the stage and carry off all the honors. Both are willing to play roles, but they find it unacceptable that certain categories of actors are authorized to play important parts while others are limited to providing the supporting cast.

Throughout the history of social psychology, the concept of role-playing has been a crucial one. The word *role* comes from *rotulus*, which in Latin means a roller, and *rotulus* comes from *rota*, which means wheel. The *rotulus* first referred to that piece of paper rolled on a cylinder upon which court cases were written, or it referred to the text of the actor written on a *rotulus*, and it is from this last meaning that we get the word *role*. But from the eleventh century on, the term *role* acquired the figurative meaning of social position or profession. So the analogy between the role of the actor and the social role is as old as the word itself, and sociologists certainly did not invent the term *role-playing*. Shakespeare is often quoted, since at least one of his characters saw the world as a stage on which we each in turn play our roles. In fact, Shakespeare uses the word *play* in a fantastic variety of meanings and contexts: "Fortune play upon thy prosperous helm";[37] "Victory, with little loss, doth play upon the dancing banner of the French";[38] "Warm life plays in that infant's veins";[39] "Those happy smiles that played on her ripe lip."[40] The adjectives he most often uses with *play* are false, foul or fair; that is, one can play fair or play false, but one always plays. Before Shakespeare, the Greek Stoics already described the world as a stage on which we each play our parts. And after Shakespeare, La Fontaine, the fabulist, also wrote that the story of the human race was like "a play of one hundred acts, with the universe as stage."

Marcel Proust was another great master in portraying the skills of role-playing. Here are two examples of his clear perception of that phenomenon. The first quotation is from *The Guermantes Way*. After one week in a small village where he has come to visit his friend St-Loup, Proust is walking back to the train station. There is no sense in staying longer there, since St-Loup has to get back to his military duties. But they had no chance to say goodbye the night before. Suddenly, Proust sees an open carriage with St-Loup standing in it, but the man does not stop to say goodbye. Instead, he performs the military salute.

> I had already observed at Balbec that, side by side with that child-like sincerity of his face, the skin of which by its transparence rendered visible the sudden tide of certain emotions, his body had been admirably trained to perform a certain number of well-bred dissimulations, and that, like a consummate actor, he could, in his regimental and in his social life, play alternately quite different parts. In one of his parts he loved me tenderly, he acted toward me almost as if he had been my brother; my brother he had been, he was now again, but for a moment that day he had been another person who did not know me and who, holding the reins, his glass screwed to his eye, without a look or a smile had lifted his disengaged hand to the peak of his cap to give me correctly the military salute.[41]

A second quotation will show how Proust understood the interaction among the many different characters that constitute our selves. The woman he loves, Albertine, has just left, and he simply cannot believe it. Before he can fully realize that Albertine has departed, his many selves each have to be informed that, really, she is gone:

And thus, at every moment there was one more of those innumerable and humble "selves" that compose our personality which was still unaware of Albertine's departure and must be informed of it; I was obliged,—and this was more cruel than if they had been strangers and had not borrowed my sensibility to pain,—to describe to all these "selves" who did not yet know of it, the calamity that had just occurred, it was necessary that each of them in turn should hear for the first time the words: "Albertine has asked for her boxes."[42]

Social psychology defines role as "the sum of cultural models in association with a given status."[43] The word *status*, in the Middle Ages, meant a set of rules imposed on members of the same craft or profession. It still has the meaning of a set of rules and regulations. It is a static concept, not at all Dionysian. The very first day in any organization, we usually know what our status is, and the bigger the organization, the more precise the definition. The term *bureaucracy* itself comes from bureau, which meant originally the room where the status of the organization was written and kept. The status is the static part, which makes it easy to be written and learned. But a role is a dynamic concept not as easily defined. Whenever we come to occupy a new status, it takes time to learn the role, to find our style, to try out new attitudes, to infuse the role with personal qualities, sometimes even to develop these personal qualities. The role slowly becomes part of our identity, whereas the status remains with the organization.

This merging of the role into the personality prompted early social psychologists like Gordon Allport in 1937 to define the personality as the integration of all the components of the status and role of the person in society.[44] In that same year, Jacob Levy Moreno, a psychiatrist who had been an actor and director, defined the neurotic as someone whose repertoire of roles is meager and dried up, which prevents him from adapting to the multiple requirements of life in society. Certain roles are not available to the neurotic because they've been repressed. To help the neurotic diversify his repertoire of behavioral responses, Moreno developed his famous technique of psychodrama. This therapeutic technique had a great success in the fifties and sixties, and though it was first developed in a clinical context, it soon got away from Moreno and was adapted to treat all kinds of personal and interpersonal

problems and widely used in organizations. Moreno's psychodrama attempted to bring theater and therapy together and as such
was very Dionysian.

When psychodrama lost its popularity, Gestalt therapy, especially under the influence of that superb ham Fritz Perls, recognized the liberating power of psychodramatic play. Perls proposed
a whole range of techniques. For example, he would suggest a
dialogue between two parts of the self: the dominant one, which
according to Perls was the "top dog," entered into conversation
with the dominated underdog. Perls wasn't above using some
props to intensify the drama: chairs, hats, pillows, tennis rackets.
Moreno's approach and Gestalt therapy both aim to help participants create a new script for their drama, to find new words,
emotions and gestures which allow them to emerge from the
power lessness of the silent, walk-on role. And since the script is a
clue to the character and the character is a clue to the myth, this
kind of play increases awareness of one's personal myth. A par-
ticipant might ask: "How can I act when my father attacks my
mother, because he is also my father? Are the words that come to
me the words of a frightened child or those of a hero defending his
mother? And how could I say to my mother that I can't serve as her
defender against her husband?" A woman might look for words
and gestures to express opposition; she may practice an aggressive
refusal to the situation that saps her energy. Another learns the
lines of a listener, like that businessman who had always given
orders and didn't know how to be a father instead of a boss for his
daughter. By role-playing, he tried out the role of attentive father.

Inevitably, the techniques of psychodrama and the exercises of
Gestalt therapy lead the group into the midst of tragedy, tragedy
interrupted by burlesque episodes, just like the Dionysian tradition. There is a point where it even looks as if there is competition:
whose life is the most tragic, whose pain the most intense, whose
problem the most complex. But then, that is exactly how tragedy
began—with a competition of lamentations. The prize went to the
author who succeeded best in moving the audience through the
pain of his heroes. Dionysos loves to show off, even in the pain
and distress of life. He gives us style in our emotional outbursts,
our rages, our childish tantrums, our love scenes, our domestic
quarrels. But there is more. He asks that we give an equal intensity, competence and sincerity to our day-to-day role-playing,

and by doing so he protects the collective life that is so vulnerable to dullness.

A Dionysian revival could come from a revisioning of our institutions from the point of view of their theatricality, staging quality and role-playing opportunities. We put a lot of effort into the financial, political, technological, and structural analyses of our institutions and organizations. But what about the dramaturgic analysis? What Goffman calls the "ritualistic reward," by which he means the opportunity one has to show off, to be seen and approved in the exercise of a role, is absent from most of our institutions, even in our schools where it would be most needed, since no young person will learn if there is no ritualistic reward.[45] Some organizations—most of all, those without much time for parties or the means to give monetary bonuses—could bestow more of these ritualistic rewards. Such rewards are needed by those whose roles are too discreet, titles too modest, uniforms too plain, spaces undecorated, jobs too simple.

Most organizations separate those who do the work and produce the goods and those who have the task of 'showing off' in public relations, representing the organization, sometimes personifying it. They get the attention, the prestige and consideration that go with the organization's success, while the others stay behind in the shade. This is not a good balance of Dionysian energies. Those of the second group acquire a frozen smile and a cold handshake from overexposure and lack of private satisfaction with a job well done, while those of the first get frustrated and depressed by the lack of recognition for the crucial role they play. They are deprived of Dionysos, even if there are plenty of parties; no amount of nightlife excitement can quite replace the Dionysian quality that is missing in the job.

We need a new appreciation of the theatrical or play-acting quality in the personality, a quality that psychology has devalued by its association with hysteria.[46] The uneasiness that is felt with what seems outrageous, over-emphatic or declamatory is often due to the frigidity of the audience and not to the theatricality of the emotions. The need to present oneself to others in a spectacular fashion only becomes hysterical when Dionysos is left out of culture. He wants to be given attention whenever we display our ornaments, be it the cap of a chef, the white wedding dress, the judge's robe, the college gown, even the jogging suit. And he wants more of this, because pleasure and vitality come from changing our repertoire and because these clothes are the costumes of our plays. As we give the God his due, we notice that besides comedy, drama and tragedy, there are also farce, melodrama, variety show, vaudeville, puppetry, fairy tales, detective drama, advertisement sketches, libretto, opera, soap opera, mystery play, miracle play, trial, news bulletins, quizzes. Dionysos can help us choose the genre or at least become aware of it. Once we feel the genre, we can attend to the dramatic structure as well—for example, that our 'domestic plays' are divided into acts or weekly episodes and include dialogues, monologues, prologues, tirades, etc.

We need more than a Dionysos who is a Devil enclosed in the Freudian Id, periodically bursting out like a steam demon from an overheated boiler. The Dionysian perspective is there to remind us that we are actors on a stage, but also that we are more or less free to rewrite roles when boredom or oppression is killing us. Dionysos is not just for parties, since there is no sense of the collective without drama, action and suspense implied in the daily routine.

No masks can belong to us definitively or exclusively; masks belong to the divinities. They are the symbols through which we communicate with the multiplicity of archetypal reality. As soon as we begin to get acquainted with the interior presences, we need a psychology that does not strive to eliminate the secondary personalities in order to reinforce the monologue of the ego. Archetypal psychology is one approach which opens up a trunkful of costumes and masks and recognizes the dramatic genius of the psyche at work in our life-stories. If we can truly accept the Dionysian perspective, we can see Dionysos as more than an ally of the hysterics, of the disheveled Bacchants and of women who are assumed to always dramatize everything. The God can become a guide, a therapist, wherever there is a role to play.

PART TWO

Hermes

Life takes on a special flavor as soon as
Hermes becomes your guide.
　　C. G. Jung and C. Kerényi, *Le Divin Fripon*

Hermes' Hat

I long felt that I was wearing Hermes' hat—a hat that made me invisible. Invisibility allowed me to see without being seen. No one paid attention to me because, consciously or not, I was taking pains to be ordinary, to be as unremarkable as possible. Neither very beautiful nor very ugly, neither a queen nor a tramp, I was gliding like the mist and I never openly opposed authority. It wasn't enough to be ordinary: I wanted to be extraordinarily ordinary. When you can go unnoticed you are truly invisible. To retire thus from power offers a privileged view of the world; the comic, the tragic and the magic sides of life can be perceived. But once you become important, socially important, you lose this hat and the immunity that ordinariness offers. That's the sign that Hermes is being left behind and another myth is being approached. I lost this hat with adulthood and social responsibilities, but I will never forget the lightness of being that comes with Hermes' hat and winged sandals.

Too often the reaction against the domination of rationalism and positivism has led to the defense of the simple-minded and ignorant, those who are excluded from the Apollo–Zeus system. But this sells short the Hermes intellect, for he is, along with Dionysos and Aphrodite, an archetype to stand up to the champions of Logos. These champions (the sharpest minds, the strongest wills, the highbrow and the powerful) are more vulnerable to the cleverness and astuteness of Hermes than to what they usually perceive as a threat—the uprising of the oppressed. Winning while appearing to lose is a strategy that a hermetic person knows how to play to advantage. The power of humor and ridicule in the face of harsh authority, the role of the court jester, the uses of flight over fight and of artful speech in negotiation—all these can be rediscovered in Hermes. David and Goliath, Tyl Eulenspiegel, Robin Hood—all have in common outwitting a powerful opponent, so that his blow strikes only water or air. Women, who are said to be wily, know these strategies, as do men who are endowed with that form of intelligence known to the Greeks as *metis,* that is, an intuitive intelligence.

To picture Hermes will require a word-portrait in small successive brushstrokes with frequent changes of perspective, because Hermes-Mercury is many-faceted, shimmering, impossible to pin down.

Who Is Communication?

If yes always meant yes and no simply no, there would be no need for theories of communication, no need for Hermes, the God of communication. The most eloquent representation of Hermes is probably the bust with two faces: one is turned toward humans, the other toward the Gods, thus symbolizing the dual meaning of all reality, the double meaning of all speech. The wisdom of a myth that makes Hermes the patron saint of liars as well as the God of communication is apparent, suggesting that communicating and lying are part of the same archetype. Loopholes, rumors, distortions, double binds, and all the notions of half-lies that many theories of communication have invented over the past twenty years have sought to describe the ambiguity and untruths that underlie human communication. Hermes, to whom we owe the art of making fire by rubbing two sticks together, expresses the same spirit when he ignites that other spark by rubbing two words or two cultures together, namely, communication.

I find it amazing that the Greek language crossed over so many natural boundaries, because the history of languages tells us that a natural barrier such as mountain, river or sea normally defines the frontier of a language. For example, the unity of Egypt or of Mesopotamia was clearly favored by geography. If we follow this reasoning, it's surprising that Greece, a chopped-up territory if there ever was one, could have attained such linguistic and cultural unity; from Cyprus to Ithaca to Sicily people could understand each other, as if language floated over mountains and bodies of water and even the most inaccessible peaks. This paradox illustrates the passion of the Greeks for communication. For them boundaries and frontiers were not obstacles but places to meet and communicate, a little like neighbors leaning over a backyard fence.

The Greeks expressed their talent for communication even when words could not be exchanged. They adopted à form of communication used by the Phoenicians, a kind of "silent trade." If, for example, I am the captain of a ship and I must get some fresh food, I might leave an assortment of gifts on the beach for the local inhabitants and then return to my ship. I come back the next day. My gifts are gone, but in their place I find fresh provisions that will help me continue my voyage and perhaps some crafted objects that I like bringing back home. If one of the objects I left is still there, I understand that the local people are not interested in it. If it was a fair trade, I might return.

The Greeks had an expression for these found objects—"a gift of Hermes," a gift that is left somewhere without knowing to whom it might be useful. Another example of this silent trade is given by the peasant who lives beside a well-traveled road: he might leave a "gift of Hermes" when he puts some bread, water and cheese in a jug at the crossroads. The hungry traveler leaves a "gift to Hermes" when he returns a few coins or other useful items in the jug after consuming the food. Adjusted to the invisible, this form of communication is based on intuiting the needs of someone who will never be seen or known. But since Hermes is "he who carries the message," it doesn't matter if the messenger is visible or not, or the language is verbal or non-verbal, literal, or symbolic, written or spoken, as long as people understand each other.

Definitely Ambiguous

The Hermes myth places communication at the intersection of all levels of language, at the point where complexity threatens to become confusion. He is comfortable somewhere between the explicit and the implicit and never tires of inventing nuances of voice, tone or gesture to place his message in the right context. Whereas Apollonian communication carries a single meaning—to be straight and clear like an arrow—communication under the sign of Hermes borrows from twisted pathways, shortcuts and parallel routes; it makes many round trips and ends up sometimes in meaningful dead ends. The paths of Hermes are multiple.

Most of our actual theories of communication were developed

around the written model. We lean toward communication that
is free of "noise," that is, free of double or implied meanings,
paradoxes, and the ambiguities that abound in a verbal exchange.
Of course, eliminating ambiguity results in more clarity, but to
"literalize" a communication robs it of the richness that complexity
provides. Writing tends to be single-voiced; the monotheistic ideal,
which is based on clarity and non-ambiguity, requires that only
one voice be heard.

But Hermes is an old God, who personified communication
before literate culture; he knows a trick or two about the complex-
ities of human exchange. When we speak with our whole being,
there has to be more than one voice at work—if we accept the
premise of archetypal psychology. To write "I owe you ten dollars"
on a piece of paper means one thing: I owe you ten dollars and
that's it. But to say "I love you" includes an "I don't love you," for
there is necessarily a person in me who doesn't love, or doesn't
always love, or a part of me that doesn't love a part of you, etc. If
the truth of writing is in its single voice, the truth of speech is in its
multiplicity, in its shadings and hesitations in tone, gesture, or
manner. Hermes' speech brings out every accent and nuance of the
"I love you"—from tenderness to fear, from a confession of de-
pendence to a desire for flight. We don't know how music produces its effect on us, and the same is true of the spoken word.
Even the most scholarly text fails to explain the fascination with
music. To understand its effect we have to hear music: no explanation will grow into notes and melody. In the same way oral communication has a mysterious effect on us; the charm is lost when
we read, for example, the transcript of a speech that enchanted us.
Human speech expresses more than words just as music expresses
more than sounds. Communication is an art: let us not forget that.

The dichotomy between speech and writing needs to be soft-
ened. Not all writing must be in the elegant scientific style of
Apollo or have the wordy precision of a lease (Hestia's domain),
because writing can be as subjective, imaginative and artful as
speech. It can be a transcription of a spoken piece: the texts of
Homer, the fables, fairy tales, or epic poems. Nowadays poetry,
literature, love letters and often journalism try to give us through
writing the same emotion we would feel if someone spoke to us
directly. (Perhaps we're compensating for the fact that we no

longer sit around in the evening and tell each other stories.) In artful literature the first person is permitted, as are fantasy, stylistic devices, and metaphor—all honoring Hermes.

Foggy and Complex

But the writing style that Descartes said had to be "clear and distinct" is the opposite of Hermes' speech. This writing, dear to Apollo as it was dear to Descartes, most perfectly realizes itself in mathematical statements which are so free of ambiguity that the relationships between mathematical symbols can be understood outside of any interpretation. Although not totally free of interpretive difficulties, scientific style tries to remain true to the linear-mathematical ideal. Even today, the very first lesson a student learns when writing a scientific report is to avoid using the first person, to stick to the facts and forget about telling a story; in order to embrace Apollo as the model of mathematical elegance the student must distance himself from Hermes.

A high-school student recently showed me a scientific report in which he compared the behavior of a laboratory mouse fed on an experimental diet of coca-cola and candy to the behavior of a control mouse nourished on whole grains and spring water. The experimental mouse died, and the control mouse lived. Enthusiastically, the teenage boy wrote the story of the experiment with such talent, such suspense, and in such an impassioned style that anyone reading it would never touch coca-cola or candy again. But his biology professor had given him a failing grade with the following comment: "This is great stuff, but you don't understand the first thing about Science. Sure, scientific texts are boring; they're not meant to provide newspaper headlines or movie scenarios. Next time, keep your literary talent, which is considerable, for your literature course and learn to stick to facts and figures. Never, never let your imagination intervene when you interpret the results." The student had mistaken the requirements of Apollo for those of Hermes. Science and storytelling don't mix.

Another God besides Apollo, namely Hestia, loves writing that is "clear and distinct." Hestia is as trustworthy and precise as a notary and as upright as a legal text. It is not for the sake of clarity alone that Hestia is so boringly careful with words, but for the sake of solidity and reliability. Hermes and Hestia as a couple complement each other in a basic way. Hermes, the diplomat, tries to read between the lines when the contract is not clear, whereas Hestia's qualities, which include a dislike for arguments, result in such precise terms that a misunderstanding is not likely to occur. Hestia's priestesses, known for their rectitude, were responsible for settling questions of inheritance; their work may be compared to that of a notary today. It's enough to read a lease to see that this type of communication requires skills attributed to Hestia rather than to Hermes, skills that relate to a clear and unambiguous type of communication.

The Mercurial Computer

Some artificial intelligence specialists like Douglas R. Hofstader[1] and Terry Winograd[2] blame the inability of computers to achieve the Faustian goal of artificial intelligence on the fact that an important part of our definition of intelligence has been overlooked in moving from oral culture to literacy and from literacy to computer-literacy—the part that allows for ambiguity. Hermes cannot be found in a setting where ambiguity is a "bug" rather than just added information.

Hofstader gives an amusing example of the overwhelming presence of ambiguity in our language. The expression "First Lady" means the wife of the president. But the ambiguity of this slippery term allows for a variety of meanings. It is used for the wife of the premier in countries without a president, or the ex-wife of a current president, or the current wife of an ex-president. "First Lady" sometimes means the president herself, if she's a woman, and in some countries where the president's widow is also the mother of the current president the expression can mean both the mother and the daughter-in-law (the wife of the current president). By restricting the definition to cover only the "spouse of a head of state," we oblige "First Lady" to mean a man if he's the spouse of a head of state (and then how can a lady be a man?). Hofstader pushes to absurd lengths all efforts to clear up this ambiguity and concludes that any definition, to be valid, has to include not only current usage but the spirit of the idea.

> Something terrible is happening to the concept as it gets more flexible. Something crucial is gradually getting buried, namely the notion that "wife of the President" is the most natural meaning, at least for Americans in this day and age. If you were told only the generalized definition, a gigantic paragraph in legalese, full of subordinate clauses, parenthetical remarks, and strings of or's—the end product of all these bizarre cases—you would be perfectly justified in concluding that Sam Pfeffenhauser, the former father-in-law of the corner drugstore's temporary manager, is just as good an example of the First Lady concept as Nancy Reagan is. When this happens, something is wrong. The definition not only should be general, but also should incorporate some indication of what the spirit of the idea is.[3]

He therefore supports the notion that, if we're going to have "intelligent" computers, it won't be by trying to make them more precisely denotative, more Apollonian, but by exploring the other side of intelligence—that is, a Hermes-type intelligence, as we would say in our mythological vocabulary.

A Wink Is a Communication

When too much clarity is required, the spirit of Hermes draws back and chooses ambiguity, not out of a stubborn preference for obscurity and paradox, but because by repudiating ambiguity one is left with only one level of meaning and only one style of communication. A wink often cancels out the seriousness of what's being said; joking and irony often allow what should not be said to be heard, because equivocality often provides a protection. To grasp the paradoxical side of Hermes, who is both God of communication and patron saint of liars and thieves, let's look at the role of lying and thievery in the part of the myth where he establishes a solid base of communication with Apollo and Zeus.

Barely one day old, Hermes steals a herd of cattle belonging to his half-brother Apollo and immediately, without embarrassment, denies it.

> "If you want,
> I'll swear a great oath

on the head of my father:
I declare that I am myself
not guilty,
nor did I see any other thief
of your cattle,
whatever cattle are, anyway—
I've only heard about them."
And while he said this,
he peeked out
from under his bright eyelids,
looking here and there.
And he whistled too,
for a long time,
like somebody listening to a lie.[4]

Apollo is nobody's fool, but he's impressed by the audacity of this newborn. He takes the case before Father Zeus, and Hermes restates his lie with even more emphasis and cheek.

"Father Zeus,
I'm going to tell you the truth.
I'm a frank person,
and I don't know how to lie.
....
I didn't take his cattle home,
though I do want to be rich.
I didn't even step over
our doorstep.
I tell you this in all honesty.
I have a great deal of respect
for the Sun and the other spirits.
And I love you.
And I dread him.
And you yourself know
that I am not guilty.
And I'll even add
this great oath:
NOT GUILTY,
by these beautiful porticoes
of the gods!

> And a day will come
> when I will pay him back
> for his reckless charges,
> even though he's stronger.
> But you, Zeus,
> help us youngsters!"
> Argeiphontes of Cyllene [Hermes]
> said this—and winked!
> And he clutched onto his blanket
> on his arm. He didn't remove it.
> Zeus let out a great big laugh
>
> ....
>
> And he ordered both of them
> to try to reconcile themselves
> to each other.

Hermes, this rascal of a child, is lying, of course, but if it's communication we're interested in—not logical thought—then we see that his words are completely effective; they get the job done. In fact, young Hermes had no access to Olympus by right; by his stunning action he forces contact first with Apollo, then with Zeus. Once he has his foot in the door, he plays his part seductively and is granted the affectionate attention of those he deceives—and a place on Olympus. That was precisely his goal, and he attained it through the spoken word, albeit deceitfully.

Business and Communication: Hermes the Merchant

> Like every rogue, Hermes lives outside the boundaries established by custom and by law. In my Hermes Psychopomp I believed I could define his domain as a "no-man's-land", that is, as a hermetic intermediary realm, surrounded by established limits where the words "to find" and "to steal" still have a distinct meaning. I subsequently added: "On the other hand, the absence of scruples alone does not constitute Hermetic action; the art and spirit of making one's way in life must also be included."
> Carl G. Jung and Carl Kerényi, *Le Divin Fripon*

We will see further along how Hermes, who stands for mediation, presides over all changes of condition, all displacements.
Commerce is a kind of mediation; goods pass from one owner to
another. But this is also true of theft, when merchandise changes
hands as surely as through commerce. The distinction between
commerce and theft bothers Apollo more than Hermes, who
doesn't see any problem in being the God of both merchants and
thieves. Let's agree with Norman O. Brown that it is more accurate
to see Hermes as a shoplifter than as a thief, for Hermes disdains
the violence often associated with a thief's personality.⁵ Thus the
Greek expression for "playing a trick (on someone)" has the same
etymology as another expression meaning "to steal without violence." But even allowing for these shades of meaning, we may
wonder why the myth suggests that commerce and theft have
something in common.

Greek merchants were pirates before turning to commerce; the
first merchants had therefore stolen what they sold. Later, after the
notion of profit replaced theft, it was still difficult for a Greek to
see profit as anything but theft. "I paid ten dollars for this object,
and I sell it to you for fifteen" or whatever amount can be negotiated through lies, fabrications, or seduction to convince the
buyer of the object's value. The merchants, as well as the money-
changers—who are commercial thieves par excellence (isn't it
sleight-of-hand with money?) and ancestors of the stock exchange
—gave a percentage of their profits to the cult of Hermes. Today's
speculators have lost the lightness and playful style of Hermes, but
they retain his skill for making extremely fast deals and we say they
"play" the stock market. Many amateur investors still play for fun
as much as for gain.

Is Stupidity a Sin?

> Dream peddlar! Comrade of black night! Daimon!
> Whimsical hinge of the floating world!
> I think I have always worshipped your quick silveriness.
> Angel of mischief, gypsy rogue with eyes of buried diamond.
>   Noel Cobb, "Hymn to Hermes"

Christian morality differs fundamentally from Greek morality
when confronted with lying and theft. For the Greek, theft is to

material things what lying is to knowledge: a deliberate trick played on someone stupid enough to be fooled. Christian morality demands "thou shalt not steal, thou shalt not bear false witness." The Hermes myth seems to suggest "thou shalt not let thyself be taken in, thou must learn how to smell a rat." For a Greek it was just as shameful to be duped as to use one's brains to dupe someone else. And so with this hazy boundary between theft and commerce and with no guarantee of integrity on either side, the genius of Hermes is to see that both parties end up feeling satisfied with the deal. This kind of paradox, where both sides feel they've won, is right up Hermes' alley.

To Hermes, "founder of trade," is attributed the invention of the scale, an instrument crucial to communication between merchant and client, since a precise measurement of quantity allows the negotiation to move on to matters of quality, margin of profit or the favors of friendship. He is also thought to have created a system of weights and measurements and, in some versions of the myth, even the alphabet and writing. It's understandable that merchants would be among the first to recognize the usefulness of writing in their transactions. The first written texts attributed to merchants do in fact look more like store inventories and grocery lists than literature.

In our fixed-price economy, communication and bargaining no longer mean the same thing as they did to a Greek businessman. Our salesmen are closer to computerized robots than to the typical merchant of ancient Greece. A "rationalized" price system holds to a minimum any need for person-to-person negotiation. A system of fixed prices takes from Hermes and gives to Apollo–Zeus; nowadays a "market economy" is held sacred rather than exchanges based on negotiation. The technocrats and politicians, high priests of the cult of Money and Order, determine in advance the outcome of an exchange between buyer and seller, making any true communication useless, even dysfunctional. Hermes' presence is no longer required. Today only independent artisans can choose to sell high to the rich, low to friends, and nothing to someone they dislike.

Negotiation makes no sense without the possibility of increasing or decreasing the margin of profit, for that's where the game is. Once in Morocco I watched a street urchin negotiate with a customer for ten minutes before selling him a handful of rusty old nails; despite the insignificance of the transaction, all of the most subtle elements of human exchange were present. To refuse to negotiate in cultures where the spirit of Hermes presides over such transactions is often taken as a personal insult, and a fixed price becomes a way of saying "I don't want to deal with you." The classic figure of the Jewish Levantine or Oriental merchant, clever and shrewd, sometimes expresses this art of exchange. But the spirit of Hermes, however crafty, doesn't rule out candor or the innocence of someone who loves playing the game and appreciates a good battle of wits. The notion of profit at any cost and the perverse influence of avarice contaminate this spirit just as surely as a fixed price or an unwillingness to communicate.

Laundering Money

Hermes, on the day of his birth, gives a masterful demonstration of a theft-transaction containing all the elements of a successful mediation: he moves from thief to decent businessman with a place of honor on Olympus. When he steals the fifty cattle from Apollo he has the feeling, as he tells his mother, that he deserves better treatment:

> "We're not going to stick around here,
> as you want, the only two
> among all the immortal gods
> without any gifts,
> without even prayers!
> It's much better
> to spend every day
> talking with the gods,
> rich, bountiful, loaded with
> cornfields, than to just
> sit around home here
> in this creepy cave.
> As for honors,
> I'm going to get in on the same ones
> that are sacred to Apollo.
> And if my father won't stand for it,
> I'll still try,

I'm capable certainly,
to be thief number one."[6]

Isn't that the motive force behind many colossal fortunes? To Hermes, Olympus is where he belongs and the theft of cattle is an act of justice! But getting the goods is only a first step. The goods must then be recognized as his; his ownership must be seen as legitimate. This way of thinking applies to many a self-made man and to those parvenus who choose to forget their origins. Their biographies illustrate the Hermes myth: the self-made man decided in his youth that the gates of some Olympus should be open to him, that justice should be done to his genius without his worrying too much about scruples. Many of these fortunes result from a series of transactions profiting from the weaknesses and defects of an economic and social system: the fortunes made during Prohibition in America, or during the crash of 1929, or lately in the stock exchange, or transactions based on a successful gimmick, a shrewd invention (Hermes' invention is a turtle turned into a lyre).

Once the coffers are filled, the question of legitimacy remains (to be admitted by Zeus). To carve out a spot in the Olympus of society you have to know how to present the right gifts to the right people (offer a lyre to Apollo), amuse those in power (make Zeus laugh), and exercise charm to win the heart of one or several women who have the power to bestow a social sanction on the newcomer (Hera). And there you have it! Time passes and no one questions anymore the legitimacy of the fortune or the social status that goes with it. An impressive proportion of great fortunes, especially American ones, come under the sign of Hermes. And it is well-known that after the Industrial Revolution the most aristocratic families of Europe, even those who scorned business deals and the nouveaux riches and America, did not hesitate to sell their daughters into advantageous marriages with Americans in order to hold on to their ancestral domains. Dirty money washed through a marriage is an old story that is alive and well today, thanks to Hermes.

Mercurial Seductiveness

One of the essential elements in any negotiation inspired by Hermes is seduction, the art of convincing the other person that the deal is to his advantage. First you have to disarm the dangerous anger of a powerful Zeus-like figure. Hermes knows better than to collide head-on with authority; it has to be outsmarted, turned aside, turned into laughter: "Zeus let out a great big laugh/ as he looked at this kid,/ who was up to no good,/ denying so well,/ so smoothly,/ that he knew anything/ about the cows."[7] Hermes is very daring, but he can't allow himself to become impolite or violent. He takes on formal authority with the informal power of seduction, laughter and ridicule. In business matters these types don't openly break the law, but they spot any weakness in the system and slide through. During the counterculture years the hippy culture used this kind of strategy. Knowing how to distract, amuse or ridicule authority can be just as effective as heroic confrontations. The same spirit could be felt at the beginning of the personal computer industry; it attracted young minds with intellectual swiftness, young geniuses with a passion for play, for gadgets, for invention, with talent for new languages and new modes of communication. It went along with a new form of thievery: computer crime. Many a youth got a lot of attention and professional opportunity by stealing data, illegally getting into a computer network, and working his way up to the Apollonian and Jupiterian bosses, impressed by his ruse. The establishment opened doors for him, as Zeus did for Hermes.

Having succeeded in getting around Zeus's aggression and in winning him over, Hermes still has to work out a basic agreement with Apollo, his half-brother. He can't hope to establish himself on Olympus without radically improving this relationship, so he works at a seduction again, this time more nearly geared to his sibling's temperament.

> It was very easy for him
> to soothe the Archer,
> son of glorious Leto,
> as he wanted to do,
> even though he was so strong.

> He took the lyre
> in his left hand,
> and tried, with the pick,
> to sound melodic.
> And under his hand
> it sounded marvelous!
> Phoebus Apollo
> was delighted, and
> burst out laughing.
> The lovely sound
> of this divine voice
> went right to his heart,
> and a sweet desire
> transfixed his spirit
> as he listened.[8]

In order to strike a good deal one has to make the other person want what one has; in this Hermes is close to Aphrodite, mistress of the most powerful attraction—sex. The language used in describing Hermes' action borrows from Aphrodite's vocabulary. The "lovely sound" of Hermes' playing "went right to [Apollo's] heart," and the "sweet desire" (for the object) "transfixed his spirit." It's in the bag! Apollo is seduced. Hermes, much reassured, has only to approach Apollo. Not only will Hermes keep what he has stolen—"this song of yours/ is worth fifty head"—but he'll ask for much more: "Since the spirit moves you/ to play the lyre,/ sing, play it,/ enjoy the fun/ that you receive from me./ But give the glory to me,/ friend."[9] Hermes, who initiated the exchange, thus obtains the cattle, the caduceus, and the protection of the three Fates.

> "I am going to make of you
> a symbol
> among immortals, and everybody else,
> and you will be trusted
> and honored in my heart.
> Furthermore,
> I'm going to give you
> a marvelous wand
> for fortune and wealth,

made of gold and triple-leafed,
and it will keep you safe
when you are carrying out
all the decrees
of favorable words and actions
which I say I know
from the voice of Zeus."[10]

What is more, Zeus offers him an exclusive contract as messenger,
making Hermes "the only recognized messenger to Hades."

Through the magic of communication, what started out as
theft becomes exchange. Hermes is transformed from thief to
businessman, from thief to diplomat, from delinquent to partner—because he knows how to awaken and then fulfill the desires
of his opponent. Even as a thief Hermes is generous; what he offers (the lyre to Apollo and the sly humor to Zeus) is of good
quality, and the relationships he establishes endure. Hermes builds
a relationship with Apollo in the same way a real businessman
keeps his best clients throughout his life.

Then the son of Maia promised,
nodding his head,
that he would never again steal
anything the Archer possessed,
and that he would never again go near
his sturdy house.[11]

Seduction is usually presented as a negative process in which the
seduced is the loser, but it can just as well be seen as a form of communication. Our negative definition illustrates to what extent the
spirit of Hermes and Aphrodite has been distorted. Norman O.
Brown notes that the phallic Hermes (represented by a stone
phallus) is not necessarily a God of fertility, as the classic Hellenists
suggest, but that the phallus may symbolize sexuality as communication and erection as the magical effect that seduction produces.

Hermes has seduced Apollo but neither one feels a loser. Their
new friendship is sealed with a nod and a promise: Hermes won't
steal from Apollo again now that the principle of exchange has
been established. Their friendship will be strong and durable. Of
all the Gods, Hermes is the least likely to attract enemies in spite of

his reputation as a brigand. He is also the only one to be warmly received by super-sensitive Hera, who might well have been angry at this son of her husband and a rival (Maia) but is nevertheless charmed by him. In one version of the myth Hera goes so far as to nurse baby Hermes at her breast, though he is not her child. Once again, can we say that he steals this milk through the power of seduction? But what woman would not be happy to nurse such a charming child?

Today commerce is no longer under the sign of Hermes, except in the Third World. There the best tradesmen have a flair for guessing who you are, what you're feeling, what your hesitation or your desire is all about; they follow you, they recognize you anywhere, they keep insisting until communication is established. These are qualities which, in the Western world, have been transferred to advertising. Despite the efforts to define advertising as a profession based on empirical methods and scientific research (marketing studies, demographics, etc.), the most gifted of these men and women are mercurial and function as artists, not as scientists.

Freedom of Speech

In mythological accounts Hermes fulfills the function of Olympian herald; that is, he carries the messages of the Gods and Goddesses to human beings. He shares this function with Iris, the young Goddess who slides down to earth on a rainbow. But Hermes, not just a delivery boy, transmits messages more like an ambassador than a postman. He interprets his mission as a diplomat might do, and he intervenes in tricky situations. For example, he negotiates Priam's right to recover the body of his son, slain by Achilles; he also takes on the delicate mission of rescuing Ulysses from the over-possessive Calypso and later from the seductive sorceress Circe.

A diplomat doesn't forget to represent his constituency, and to do his job well he must be free to make adjustments in any given situation. Hermes and Athena are present whenever diplomacy occurs. Athena sees that the principles of justice that she incarnates are not disregarded, while Hermes makes sure all parties have expressed themselves and been heard. The heralds of ancient Greece not only served as emissaries abroad but were organizers and cheerleaders, so to speak, of civic and military groups at home. Today they'd be called chairpersons, arbitrators, moderators, facilitators, or mediators. They maintained order by "commending the folk to be silent" so that "all, those in the last row as well as those in the first row," might be heard.[12] When the assembly was so crowded that it seemed a "bee buzz"[13] and when "uproar ruled the assembly,"[14] several heralds joined forces: "the heralds—nine—kept calling aloud to restrain them, if ever from clamor they would desist, from tumult. . . ."

The herald used Hermes' scepter, the caduceus, to recognize those who wanted to speak from the floor. "They received the sceptre from the clear-voiced heralds and each person rises in turn to express himself, sceptre in hand."[15] His function was not to judge or pass sentence when differences erupted but to calm things down and maintain an atmosphere that allowed each person to express himself, scepter in hand, so that a decision might be reached. In ancient Greece the role of the herald was considered sacred and was respected and obeyed. Small white pieces of cloth were attached to the caduceus so that the bearer could be recognized everywhere, even in the enemy camp; the flags signified a truce or a pause allowing for discussion or delivery of a message. This gave rise to the white flag which serves the same purpose today, signifying that negotiations or a truce or some sort of communication will take place.

As a chairperson, the herald does not and cannot take sides in quarrels or disputes; he sees to it that confrontations, judgments, negotiations, contracts, etc., are carried out according to form, to protocol and procedural code. When, for example, Hector and Ajax, the two tenacious warriors, are on the point of "striking at close range with their swords," Hermes only places his scepter firmly between them and the fighting ceases:

> Cease, children, your warring combat. Both of you are dear to Zeus, the cloud-gatherer. You are both equally valiant warriors. We all know that. But look, night has fallen, now it is best to obey the night.[16]

In this example, it makes sense for the opponents to stop fighting, because night has come, and ancient Greek soldiers usually stopped fighting at nightfall. Hector and Ajax do not resume fighting the next day: they had fought "for as long as their hearts were full of rancor" and, having exhausted their anger, "they parted friends."

Managing communications in a democratic manner gets more complex as the number of participants increases. With judicious use of the caduceus and with their intuitive grasp of group processes, the heralds took responsibility for the flow of communication even in very large gatherings. They knew a thing or two about group psychology, group cohesiveness and group decision making. Just as a contemporary chairperson sees to it that value judgments and criticisms do not inhibit the free expression of opinions, the Greek herald, by handing out the scepter, granted temporary immunity to a speaker. This democratic ritual has been part of our culture ever since. Freedom of speech is Hermes' gift. Communication is Hermes' grace.

Whenever negotiations break down, whenever there are hidden agendas and tiresome intrigues, whenever a committee suffers from such an overdose of procedure that structure devours content, Hermes is offended. He gets his revenge by sowing confusion and stopping the flow of ideas so that in the end nothing is really said. Fifteen years of regular attendance at required faculty meetings of my university department—the department of communication!—have convinced me that the absence of Hermes means that power games and personal agendas will take the place of communication. When controlling the procedure itself is an exercise of power, the resolutions which have been formally adopted can be scuttled by passive resistance, absenteeism and ill will. Hermes' spirit is lost.

The caduceus is a staff around which are entwined two serpents of equal but opposing force—a symbol of equilibrium through the integration of contrary forces. It's a good representation of what a group leader should do, fostering the expression of all opinions, especially when they contradict each other (the two serpents), and seeking through discussion and negotiation a new equilibrium, an agreement or a compromise. Hermes' staff positioned between two fighting serpents eloquently illustrates arbitration. But the staff as axis can also be taken as a symbol of democracy. Stimulating the expression of divergent points of view, democracy fosters their integration around an axis so that a new synthesis, a new deal, a new proposition capable of reconciling opposites may emerge. Even though the heralds belonged to the Homeric period and the concept of democracy to the classical era, Hermes, the herald incarnate, prefigures the democratic spirit in the sense that free speech, confrontation and discussion are a prerequisite to democracy. The Sophists of the archaic period, along with the classical orators, carried on Hermes' work and brought us to the doorstep of democracy.

A true democracy involves more than the right to vote. A certain quality of communication is needed, as well as the freedom to try to influence decisions. The "popular democracy" in the Soviet Union does not strike us as a true one; the dice appear to be loaded since the candidate is chosen by the Party. But sometimes the control exercised by financial interests or by a social class in our own elections is just as anti-democratic, and we are seemingly not offended. We are extremely sensitive, however, to any threat to freedom of speech or freedom of the press, because we know that the vote in itself does not insure democracy.

These freedoms, fundamental to democracy, are best expressed in what we call "free" journalism. Journalism attracts children of Hermes because a good journalist, aside from a certain crafty intensity, possesses the art of eliciting information as well as telling about it. Restless and intuitive, he must often dissemble or even steal information or perhaps lie about his identity to get to the bottom of the story. The true journalist, like Hermes, champions the democratic ideal; he reveals cover-ups and finds leaks in the system. This spying on the establishment constitutes a civilian watchdog system and can sometimes topple entrenched power. Hermes persists in speaking out more or less candidly about what he sees, right alongside the Zeus establishment (legislative and executive) and its Apollonian allies (scientific and military technology). A Hermes renaissance could serve to oppose "Big Brother": communication as an antidote to domination.

A Blow against Democracy

During the Peloponnesian War, in which democratic Athens opposed a rigid Sparta, a group of citizens who didn't share the democratic ideal mounted a demonstration in Athens. They protested by mutilating, in secret and at night, the quadrangular Hermes stone statues which stood at doorways, gates and sanctuaries everywhere in the city. The same night this group ridiculed the mysteries of Eleusis, which were universally deemed secret and sacred. Thucydides tells us that the people interpreted this insult to Hermes as a conspiracy: "the Athenians took the affair very seriously, seeing in it an indication of a revolutionary plot to bring down the democratic regime."[17]

It was never known for certain who was responsible for the sacrilege. However, the conflict seemed to be between the young militant sons of rich Athenian families, influenced by antidemocratic and Platonic ideas, and the polytheistic majority, which was attached to the popular divinities—Hermes, Demeter, Dionysos, Aphrodite. As for the parodies, Alcibiades (Socrates' lover) was held responsible, confirming that the conflict was both religious and political in content. The men who wanted to take over the leadership of the "popular party" relied on the deposition of tradesmen and domestics who implicated Alcibiades, well-known for his anti-democratic behavior and his contemptuous attitude toward popular rituals.

Historians place little importance on this event, considering it bizarre and insignificant. It is, in a way: since only male citizens could vote and women, slaves and aliens were excluded, why were all these people so anxious to defend democracy? If the people saw the desecration of the Hermes statues as a blow against democracy, could it be that a democracy associated with Hermes favors those who know how to talk, to persuade, to communicate even without the vote? Aesop, a writer and a slave, likes to quote Hermes because he associates him with the right to intercede, to plead a cause, to criticize and even to blame rulers without fear of being censured or punished.

The people's reaction to the destruction of the Hermes statues reveals a close connection between a certain form of popular democracy and polytheism. Plato understood the people's attachment to their divinities, their need for cults and superstitions, their respect for feminine divinities. But his idea was to use this "polytheistic fallacy" to control the ignorant peasantry and to install state mythologists to manipulate the imaginative life of the people.

Another utopist, Jean-Jacques Rousseau, even though committed theoretically to the common good, came to the same kind of Big Brother conclusion: the people must be manipulated for their own good. Such centralized control is anathema to Hermes, and one way to oppose it is to support free speech and let the children say that the emperor has no clothes if indeed they see none.

Seductive Speech: Rhetoric

A good orator can convince almost anyone of anything. The art of persuasion in public speaking, that is, the art of the sophist, engenders a speech that is sprinkled with catchwords and appealing phrases, with the goal of winning over the listener. The sophist plays with words the way a juggler juggles objects. Both are under the sign of Hermes and share his lively mercurial spirit. The unexpected effects of a sophist's speech spring from a quick, intuitive intelligence and a well-honed verbal reflex. The masters of rhetoric in ancient Greece cared little about defending the truth of a thesis but rather concentrated on the skill and persuasive force of the delivery.

They taught their students to defend an idea and then to defend its opposite in order to acquire verbal flexibility unattached to context. Rhetoric is a verbal pirouette, a Hermes-like acrobatic turn, which is distinct from Athena's dialectic, even though both aim to convince and carry the day. Her argument is more formal, proceeding from the logic of the conflict of opposites (thesis and antithesis) which is then transcended by a new inclusive category, synthesis. Each divinity has its own persuasive style. Dionysos expresses himself through song, chants, groans and bursts of laughter; Zeus metes out justice, gives orders, makes rulings. Apollo, precise and knowledgeable, puts together brilliant logical proofs. Hestia's expression is spare and straightforward.

Unlike Apollo, Hermes is not interested in proving what he advocates. He wants to win over the audience and get the applause, even if it means twisting the truth. Great orators who have that magic power of persuasion are all very quick on their feet and know intuitively what to say and what not to say. One of the finest speeches inspired by Hermes is the one addressed to Achilles by the aged Priam when he requests the body of his son Hector so that he can give him full burial honors. Hermes, after leading Priam up to Achilles' camp, tells him what he must say to touch the warrior:

Thou, though, enter at once and clasp the knees of Pelides, and for the sake of his sire, for the sake of his fair-haired mother, and for his child, that thou mayest move the spirit within him.[18]

Storytelling

People who are totally deprived of Hermes-like qualities seem dull and boring. Their stories are insipid and numbing (but unfortunately too irritating to fall asleep over). We've all listened to preachers, professors or acquaintances who make us want to run every time we see them for fear of dying of boredom. The Hermes archetype has never been activated in them, and their memories seem scantily furnished. We want to shake them to produce that psychological quickening so typical of Hermes. Next to them, the person who can remember vividly and can tell and retell the same story without ever losing its freshness seems wonderful indeed.

The myth tells us that Hermes possessed the power to put to sleep and the power to wake up. That is what a storyteller does: to guide the listener into a mythic world close to dream and sleep (children have been put to sleep with stories since time began) and yet to arouse enough interest and curiosity so that he forgets his surroundings and can enter into the world of the story. A good horror story produces gooseflesh, an erotic tale arouses desire, a tale of wonder lifts the mind, and a funny story provokes laughter— all signs that the narrator has succeeded in communicating a different reality.

Our stories may also arise from a voyage, "elsewhere" taking the place of "once upon a time." Voyages put wings on our sandals, like Hermes'. But it's not enough just to have something to talk about; the words must make a connection between the inner world of the listener and the "elsewhere" of the teller. The inspired storyteller, with shining eyes and velvet voice, sometimes adds, leaves out, adjusts the facts, but he would never admit to lying, because the mythic sense, the emotional meaning that he wants to communicate, can remain the same even when he changes things around. The true storyteller, like the artist, takes liberties with the facts and changes his story from one telling to another, but he is only satisfied with his work when he succeeds in communicating the experience to which he bears witness.

If Hermes is not on the side of facts, it's not just because he's the God of liars, for if he were nothing but a liar no one would be interested in his stories. He is, par excellence, a God of mythic thought, more interested in the truth of symbols than the truth of facts. As Messenger of the Gods, he brings the fundamental message of all Gods—which is myth. The Renaissance recognized his myth-bringing function by attributing its source book of mythic wisdom to Hermes Trismegistus. He is also, let us not forget, a follower of Mnemosyne.

> And the first of the gods
> that he commemorated with his song
> was Mnemosyne, Mother of Muses,
> for the son of Maia
> was a follower of hers.[19]

Walter J. Ong,[20] Jack Goody[21] and Erick Havelock[22] have challenged the accepted theory which held that storytellers, as memory-receptacles of an entire people, reproduce their stories word for word. Goody's experiments are revealing.[23] Using a tape recorder, he collected the tales of African storytellers over a long period of time asking them every few years to retell the same story. Noting variations in stories that were supposed to be exact repetitions, he confronted them with their different interpretations. They were insulted. They denied any difference in the stories and blamed the tape recorder, as though it were absurd to trust a mechanical recording of a story over a human storyteller who has trained himself to keep the basic tales alive. They were true servants of Hermes.

The Feminine Intelligence of Hermes

> Women are by nature devious.
> Euripides, *Iphigenia*

Metis is the name the Greeks gave to an intuitive intelligence often attributed to women. A statement like "there's no understanding women" reflects an ignorance of metis, for the path of metis is sinuous, unpredictable, and unsettling for those who have none of it in themselves. Synonymous with prudence, reflection and wisdom, metis is the opposite of deductive knowledge and is contrary to the linear logic of Apollo. Essentially an intuitive quality, it is what we might today call "situational intelligence." Rooted in an inner knowledge, an intuitive perception of contexts, and a sense of intimacy with all of nature's ways, it belongs to mythic thought, where logic does not apply. This is Hermes' brand of intelligence which he gets from the Goddess Metis herself and shares with the great seductresses Aphrodite, Pandora, Ariadne, the sorceress Medea, the magician Circe, the strategist Athena (daughter of Metis) and many Greek heroes, especially Ulysses.

Metis, Goddess of wisdom, who according to Hesiod "knew more than all the gods and men put together," was Zeus's first wife. Now Zeus, warned that his wife's intelligence could be passed on to their offspring, thereby producing children superior to himself, decided not to risk being dethroned. He swallowed Metis before she could give birth to the formidable Athena so that the royal power would never belong to anyone other than Zeus among the living Gods. Here is a myth typical of the patriarchal turn of mind. Zeus swallows his wife because she is too strong, and feminine intelligence, from then on called intuition, is imprisoned in the belly of Zeus. A shadow was cast on the notion of intuition that persists to this day because it is a kind of "gut" intelligence which, although not exclusively, tends to characterize women: Hermes has it.

A God who is male by sex but feminine in spirit, Hermes is constantly scheming with Aphrodite, who has metis. When Aphrodite's husband Hephaistos surprises her in bed with her lover Ares, he calls upon the whole of Olympus to witness the treachery of his wife. Hermes manages to intervene on her behalf to save her reputation.

He is also the one who gives Pandora her lies and her deceitful nature, to the great discomfort of men who are enamored of clarity but bound by the weakness of the flesh. Hephaistos, the handyman-artisan of Olympus, created this extraordinarily beautiful virgin out of clay and water, but Hermes gave her her sly intelligence, her cunning and her way with words.

> But into her heart Hermes, the guide, the slayer of Argos, put lies,
> and wheedling words of falsehood, and treacherous nature, made

her as Zeus of the deep thunder wished, and he, the god's herald,
put a voice inside her, and gave her the name of woman.[24]

This gift from Zeus to Epimetheus (brother of Prometheus)
was meant to entrap Man. The idea was to seduce Man with
her beauty but to give her such a twisted character that Man
could never control her. For Pandora is a liar who combines
treachery with seduction and confronts Man with his own weakness. With the box (or more accurately the jar) in which Pandora
was placed, Zeus avenged the gift of fire given to Man by Prometheus. As Hesiod comments: "all men shall fondle this, their
evil, close to their hearts, and take delight in it."[25] Much has been
made of the hateful side of Pandora and the sexist nature of this
myth. But I like it. Pandora represents rather well one aspect of
patriarchal ideology: the man who forgets his humanity and af-
fects Promethean airs sooner or later is faced with a woman, a
Pandora, whom he can't control, a woman who calls him back to
his humanity. Her cunning prevents Man from imagining he's a
God, and I believe that's a sensible gift, given the arrogance of
men. A feminist reading of this myth would suggest a return to
Pandora every time Promethean male heroism encroaches on feminine territory.

This myth reveals the two-faced nature of Hermes. The opportunity to lie comes with speech; wherever there is Man, there can
be Pandora, and Hermes himself sees to it that she is a liar. But
Pandora is gifted by the Gods. She weaves well—"Athene was to
teach her her skills, and how to do the intricate weaving"[26]—and
she is lovely to look at—"Aphrodite was to mist her head in
golden endearment and the cruelty of desire and longings that
wear out the body"—for Hephaistos created her in the image of
the immortal Aphrodite. Pandora, not Hermes, is an image of the
complexity and ambivalence of life where feelings are almost
always mixed feelings.

Metis and Technique

The technical ingenuity required to invent a corkscrew or a zipper or a toaster is of a totally different order than what is needed
to build a bridge or an aqueduct. In fact, at least three different

attitudes toward technique can be discussed. First of all, there is the technique of the engineer trained in the school of Apollo. This is a deductive method, scientific and well thought out, and metis takes second place to mathematics and physics. For it is Apollonian qualities that guarantee that the bridge or the dam will hold, that the rocket will lift off, that a certain domination over the natural world can be achieved. The engineer does not wait for inspiration; he calculates, measures and verifies. Here technique is closer to scientific knowledge than to ingenuity; in the spirit of Apollo, technique becomes technology.

Second is the attitude of the artisan, as typified by Hephaistos and Athena. Metis is part of it, but it's mostly patience and sustained effort, along with manual dexterity and the qualities traditionally associated with craftsmanship. The mode of production is personalized, and its objective is as much aesthetic as functional. Today's artisans who work for themselves or on commission, who have a taste for "inspired" work, share the spirit of hard-working Hephaistos and ingenious Athena.

Third, there is the Hermes technique which is inventive, intuitive, non-critical, with plenty of room for play. A restless imagination presides over the inventiveness of Hermes: "I come upon whatever I am looking for in everything indifferently, since I don't know what I am looking for."[27]

Whenever an inventor describes his breakthrough as a flash or a vision or a crazy idea, he confirms the presence of Hermes. This is the way Hermes constructed the first lyre:

> There
> he found a turtle
> and it brought him
> lots of fun:
> Hermes was the first
> to manufacture songs
> from the turtle he encountered
> outside the door,
> as it was eating
> the splendid grass
> outside the door of their home.
> It moved along
> with an affected step.

The son of Zeus,
the helper,
looked at it,
then burst out laughing,
and said this:
"What a great sign,
what a help this is for me!
I won't ignore it.
Hello there,
little creature,
dancing up and down,
companion at festivals,
how exciting it is
to see you."
....
Then, just as a thought
runs quick
through the heart of a man
whose troubles pile up
and shake him, or
when you see a twinkling
spin off the eyes,
just like that
the glorious Hermes
started thinking
about words and actions.
He measured
and cut stalks of reed
and fixed them in
by piercing through
the back of the shell
of the turtle.
Full of ideas,
he stretched cow-hide over it,
and put in the bridge,
and fitted the two arms,
and stretched out
seven harmonious chords
of sheep-gut.[28]

The technical creativity of a Hermes comes from an openness reflected in his attitude toward the tortoise. There is something hermetic in those who create original decors made up of found objects, recycling with ingenuity whatever falls into their hands: "What a help this is for me! I won't ignore it," Hermes says of the tortoise-shell. In short, Hermes is opportunistic, an acceptable quality when dealing with material things. It is less well tolerated when expressed in relationships. And yet opportunism is as basic to Hermes' psychology as his technical skill; the word itself means an "opening" and is characteristic of a mercurial spirit. James Hillman has grasped the archetypal quality of opportunism and its connection to Hermes, the youngest God, the mischievous little brother, the eternal child. Starting from this one quality, he retraces the psychology of puer, and inevitably we recognize Hermes:

> "Chance" and "system" are other words for puer and senex. Senex consciousness lives from the plotted curve of expectations. Establishment requires predictability: we must plan for eventualities, provide for the future, run no risks. Within a senex cosmos chance will be either reduced to meaninglessness by calling it "random events" or fit into order as "statistical probabilities." Otherwise, chance becomes chancey and those who follow it chancers; opportunity becomes opportunism and those who follow opportunists— major charges against the puer. Puer existence, however, is based on opportunities and therefore an archetypal aspect of existence is reflected through this style. What we may learn about opportunism may tell us as well something about the puer aspect of existence itself.[29]

Hermes' inventiveness is playful, but that doesn't mean it's not useful. The process that leads to invention is a creative play-period with material objects rather than a desire to dominate the world. It has to do with how a creator looks at his object. Looking at the tortoise-shell, Hermes "burst out laughing" and "picking up/ this lovable toy/ with both hands/ he returned to his house,/ carrying it with him."[30] All mercurial inventions conceal a playful aspect, and those who make hermetic gadgets as well as those who enjoy them thereby express their connection to Hermes.

Metis reaches its zenith when Hermes invents fire. Not Promethean fire but domestic fire, which Hermes creates by rubbing together two sticks of different quality—a hard wood, phallic and in the form of a rod, twirled against a piece of hollowed soft wood forming a receptacle.

> Then he gathered up
> a lot of wood,
> and tried to figure out
> the art of fire:
> he took a laurel branch
> and struck it up and down
> on a pomegranate stick
> in his other hand.
> It breathed
> warm smoke.
> So it was Hermes
> who was the first
> to come up with fire,
> and the way to make it.[31]

He doesn't steal this fire; he makes it himself. It's a technique. Hermes is a chthonian God, a very ancient one. According to myth he was born in a dark cavern. Would this be a mythic way of remembering that fire refined the human's carnivorous nature? "But then glorious Hermes himself/ wanted some of the sacred meat:/ immortal or not,/ the delicious smells/ troubled him." Dionysos gave wine to humanity, Athena olive oil, Demeter bread, Aphrodite berries and honey, and Hermes follows up with the taste of roasted meat—every divinity contributing to the polytheistic banquet.

In the same way that a sense of intimacy with the animal world makes domestication possible, a close connection with the world of objects produces a technically inventive mind. You have to know an animal well to tame it. Hermes shares with Artemis and Demeter the job of protecting and domesticating animals. I once saw a boy of about nine, a mercurial child wonderfully endowed with metis, tame a wild dog and hitch it to a sled. I asked him how he managed to do it and he said: "I spent a lot of time watching him, we became friends, and then he wanted to play with me. I think he wanted to try out my sled, so I made him a harness."

Plutarch tells with feeling about how skillfully Alexander tamed Bucephalus, the horse who became his lifelong friend:

There came a day when Philoneicus the Thessalian brought Philip a horse named Bucephalus, which he offered to sell for thirteen talents. The king and his friends went down to the plain to watch the horse's trials, and came to the conclusion that he was wild and quite unmanageable, for he would allow no one to mount him, nor would he endure the shouts of Philip's grooms, but reared up against anyone who approached him. The king became angry at being offered such a vicious animal unbroken, and ordered it to be led away. But Alexander, who was standing close by, remarked, "What horse they are losing, and all because they don't know how to handle him, or dare not try!" Philip kept quiet at first, but when he heard Alexander repeat these words several times and saw that he was upset, he asked him, "Are you finding fault with your elders because you think you know more than they do, or can manage a horse better?" "At least I could manage this one better," retorted Alexander. "And if you cannot," said his father, "what penalty will you pay for being so impertinent?" "I will pay the price of the horse," answered the boy. At this the whole company burst out laughing, and then as soon as the father and son had settled the terms of the bet, Alexander went quickly up to Bucephalus, took off his bridle, and turned him towards the sun, for he had noticed that the horse was shying at the sight of his own shadow, as it fell in front of him and constantly moved whenever he did. He ran alongside the animal for a little way, calming him down by stroking him, and then when he saw he was full of spirit and courage, he quietly threw aside his cloak and with a light spring vaulted safely onto his back. For a little while he kept feeling the bit with the reins, without jarring or tearing his mouth, and got him collected. Finally, when he saw that the horse was free of his fears and impatient to show his speed, he gave him his head and urged him forward, using a commanding voice and touch of the foot.

At first Philip and his friends held their breath and looked on in an agony of suspense, until they saw Alexander reach the end of his gallop, turn in full control, and ride back triumphant and exulting in his success. Thereupon the rest of the company broke into loud applause, while his father, we are told, actually wept for joy, and when Alexander had dismounted he kissed him and said: "My boy, you must find a kingdom big enough for your ambitions. Macedonia is too small for you."[32]

Technical ingenuity involves a certain domestication of an object. The form is tamed, its qualities are appreciated, it begins to reveal itself, it has something to say. Just as a hammer teaches us what to do with nails, every object has something to communicate to us.

Mythic Thought

Reflecting on Hermes allows us to appreciate the kind of intelligence that operates through association, analogy, and intuition. Metis loves repetition and delicate shading; it would rather accumulate than analyze—and this is what makes myths enjoyable.

The mythic thought of Hermes—and all the Goddesses with metis—was just as valid to the ancient Greeks as Apollo's reason. Unfortunately, since the Logos concluded that the world is rational and that human reason reflects it perfectly, we've lost touch with mythic thought. We suspect, however, that the world is too complex and too profound to be explained by human reason alone, that the universe cannot be contained in an Apollonian formula, that a universe with contradictions is not necessarily an absurd one. Mythic thought suggests that the world is complex, not that it is confused. The ambiguity of myth resembles the ambiguity of dreams; both bring multiple meanings to awareness. Their significance cannot be plumbed in a single interpretation, however intelligent it may be, and thus dream and myth reflect more of the world's deepest reality than, for example, a theorem, which is useful when a single value is sought. To put an end to structuralist monomania, we must stop treating myth only as a mathematical statement and learn to treat it like a dream, or a painting, or a person.

Jung's method of interpreting dreams draws inspiration from mythic thought, whereas Freud's is more deductive. Jung's mercurial personality is well-known[33] and his close relationship to mythic thought very evident; he seems to have been incredibly endowed with metis. Like Hermes he is an "initiator of dreams." But there is more. At a crucial moment in his relationship to Freud, for him a paternal figure with the qualities of both Apollo and Zeus, Jung resorted to a lie:

> While I was trying to find a convenient answer to Freud's questions, I was suddenly troubled by an intuition concerning the role that the subjective factor may play in understanding psychology. This intuition was so strong that I had only one thought: to get out of this involved situation as fast as possible, which I easily did by means of a lie. It was not elegant, nor morally defensible, but if I had not done it, I risked a definitive quarrel with Freud, and I felt unable to undertake this for many reasons.[34]

Not only is the lie characteristic of Hermes, but Jung also defends here his therapeutic perspective, rooted in his metis, as compared to Freud's more Apollonian approach.

> It was not Freud's dream. It was mine. And in a flash, I understood its message. This conflict illustrates a central point in the analysis of dreams. It is less a technique that one may learn to apply by following the rules than a dialectical exchange between two personalities. If one treats analysis as a mechanical technique, the psychic personality of the dreamer with all its individuality will be incapable of expression, and the therapeutic problem will be reduced to the simple question: who will dominate, the analyst or the dreamer?[35]

Jung insists on communication and rejects domination of any sort in a therapeutic relationship; his method for the interpretation of dreams assumes that the patient will develop his own metis and that the therapist will act as guide, not as master. Non-directive and client-centered long before Carl Rogers popularized this approach, Jung wrote:

> I wanted the process of healing to be born from the patient's own personality, not from a suggestion made by me. The effects of the latter would have been short-lived. My aim was to protect and maintain intact both the dignity and the liberty of my patient, so that he could fashion his life according to his own desires.[36]

Rafael López-Pedraza, in *Hermes and His Children*, throws a new light on the therapeutic relationship in a mercurial context.[37] He says that, when the therapist is so impeccable in manner that he claims for himself all possible dignity, then his client is left with only one option, indignity. Whereas therapy should be the one place where all the humiliations, lies and treacheries that are part of human nature can be expressed.

To return to Jung, the fact that he lied to Freud, that he had long periods of turbulence in his life, that he had a mistress in a very moralistic era confirms for us the hermetic qualities which characterize his work, in contrast to Freud, the stern and frustrated father.

Perhaps it is this absence of Hermes-like qualities that leads so many psychoanalysts to believe that dream interpretation implies replacing the dream with its explanation. Instead of looking at the dream images as one would look at paintings in a museum, one is lecturing about them. Whether it be psychological, sociological or historical, the explanation fails to plumb the depth of the symbolic images. Intuition (mysterious in itself, since we still don't know what it is and how it works) is called for.

The term *demystify* usually means to uncover a ruse, to unmask a treachery. When myth is used in the sense of a lie, of course we must demystify with all haste, denouncing not the myth itself but its literal interpretation which can only be misleading. But only those who've made it literal are deceived. If we truly believe in the Immaculate Conception, we feel vaguely deceived when we stop believing that the Virgin could have been biologically impregnated by a spirit disguised as a bird. But if Christian dogma had not insisted that these stories be accepted as faith, if it had allowed them to be treated as metaphor and myth, having to do with the evolution of our collective consciousness, we wouldn't be in such need of demystification.

There is another way to miss out on mythic thought, besides being literal: identifying the myth with an impenetrable mystery. We speak, for example, of the "mystery of Love" or the "mystery of Femininity" in a way that is a refusal to understand, ruling out intuitive intelligence, rejecting metis. Myth is confused with the Christian "mystery" which was not meant to be understood with metis but believed in with faith. Christian faith forced us to give up metis.

Unlike us, the Greeks were sceptics. They had little faith. Their

Gods did not require a credo, "I believe." The religious myths belonged to them just as my dreams belong to me; they knew that the myths were collective "dream images" not to be taken literally. If a dream (a myth) brings me fresh understanding of a personal situation, why turn my back on it?

Some Christians today treat Christian mythology for what it is: one of the greatest, most powerful mythologies in Occidental history. They remain attached to it because the images still speak to their hearts or because they are fond of certain rituals. They substitute mythic thought for mystery and faith and behave more like Pagans than Christians; that is, their traditional faith is gone, but for them stories of Christian mythology are still charged with emotion. They remain attached by ceremony and sentiment. I've talked to young students who consider themselves very attached to the Christian faith, but I've noticed that it isn't the traditional concept of God that sustains them. Rather, their imagination needs church bells, candles, the smell of incense, the music of a children's choir, the many rituals of life transition: baptism, marriage, death. These rituals have little to do with theology, cardinals and Popes. They are experienced through participation; they afford communication with invisible powers. If asked, these Pagan-Christians shrug off the question of faith ("I just like to be in church"), and they go there with metis. Theologically, they behave more like "born again Pagans" than "born again Christians"; they are mythologizing what was meant as dogma.

The Healer

Hermes' metis is most useful in the treatment of psychosomatic illnesses. If a symptom can be considered to be a message, then therapy is communication. The therapist needs metis to negotiate with the patient's unconscious, to uncover its schemes, and to recognize the multiple disguises of the symptom.

Even if we've never thought much about a caduceus and never noticed that it is before our eyes every day on prescription forms, pharmacy signs and business cards, we nevertheless have an image, a conception of medicine. That image has been forged by agreeing with or opposing the principles and values established in ancient Greece, summed up in the symbol of the caduceus.

Two kinds of medicine have come down to us: one from Hermes and one from Apollo, both represented by the caduceus. The first (Hermes') is shamanistic medicine, the second (Apollo's), scientific medicine. Both are essential to us. Like the symbol of the serpent or the tree, the caduceus is so old that years could be spent on an inventory of all possible meanings moving across the cultures of India and Greece and passing through China and Egypt. Sometimes the staff represents the axis of the universe, and the two serpents, the contrary forces that swirl around it. The organization of these forces around an axis brings equilibrium, because without organization there is chaos. The caduceus thus becomes a symbol of peace, as opposed to war, of course, but also as opposed to chaos, disorder and destruction. This peace is attained by balancing contrary forces, not because negative forces do not exist.

Sometimes the staff represents a phallus. The two serpents coupled around this phallus are the masculine symbol of fertility, of life as a moment of balance between birth and death. Just as often seen as a feminine symbol, the staff becomes a tree, itself a symbol of the ancient feminine divinity which shelters and nourishes life. The Hindu caduceus, for example, as well as the Mesopotamian one, is associated with the sacred tree, source of life.

As for the serpent, doubled on the caduceus, it is one of humanity's oldest representations of divinity and appears in all nature religions. If one looks at all the different interpretations given the serpent throughout history, it's apparent that its meaning lies close to what science today attributes to the reptilian brain—namely, the most primitive reactions of our organism, those involving survival, sexuality, combat and the protection of the young. The problems that these instinctive responses pose for the moral order are summed up in the symbol of the serpent, which is both good and evil. The negative side—living only by one's instincts, guided only by one's reptilian brain—is more or less the equivalent, morally, of crawling through life without lifting up one's head to look around. The positive side of the symbol is the secret of regeneration and the wisdom we grant the serpent. Long before our evolutionary theories in biology, the serpent was considered among the most ancient of creatures, associated with the forces of Night and the Mother Goddess, primeval sources of the mystery of life.

We know what Christianity did to the serpent symbol, and we understand that Mary's act of crushing his head symbolizes Christianity's depreciation of instinctive life and the values associated with Greek paganism. (The major Greek divinities had their serpent forms: Zeus, Dionysos, Apollo, Hermes, Asclepius, Hades, Athena, Demeter.) During the Middle Ages many sects, including the Alchemists and the Gnostics, continued to defend the serpent and what it stood for, but they did so in secret. In the Greek era two wings were mounted on the two serpents, supporting the idea of a balance between underworld (the serpents) and upperworld (the wings). It is this caduceus that carries the most meaning in the development of Western medicine, and it represents the fundamental prescription of Greek medicine: equilibrium and holism.

Scientific medicine started with Apollo and his son Asclepius. The legend of Asclepius, God of medicine, is of later origin than the Hermes myth and concerns an excellent physician who succumbed to the immoderate temptation of resuscitating the dead. The God Hades, whose job was to receive the dead into the underworld, noticed that his clientele was diminishing and, feeling threatened, complained to Zeus. The great dispenser of justice struck Asclepius down with lightning for being too ambitious. After his death this legendary hero was promoted to the rank of a divinity, as patron of doctors. The Romans adopted him, calling him Aesculapius. Asclepius has the attributes of the caduceus, and legend makes him a son of Apollo, the God who governed the expansion of scientific thought. It is Apollo, not Hermes, who was recognized by the first doctors of the scientific tradition as their true patron, and they made their vows to him in the famous Hippocratic oath, which begins thus:

> I swear by Apollo, the physician, by Hygia and by Panacea, by all the Gods and Goddesses, whom I take as witness, that I shall fulfill, with all my strength and ability, the following pledge. . . .

But before proceeding with scientific medicine, let's return to the Hermes caduceus, which had been for a long time the only medicine, consisting in charms and potions, baths and rituals, pilgrimages and trials, magic and incantations. At Epidaurus, fasts, purifying rites, hygiene and rest were considered therapeutic, along with religious practices. After participating in certain ceremonies, the sick person slept in the temple and saw in his dreams the cause of his illness and what could bring about its healing. The next day he recounted his dream to a priest who interpreted it and prescribed the treatment. The patient expressedthanks by throwing gold into the temple fountain. This shamanistic medicine is symbolized by Hermes, God of communication and God of magicians. Hermes' staff stands for health seen as a balance established amid contrary forces rather than as a fixed state of being. This concept of health retains the ambivalence and flexibility of Hermes and assumes that the therapist will use metis to negotiate with the patient, who consciously wishes to get better and unconsciously may wish the opposite. Any shift in equilibrium must provide some obvious physical gains and satisfy the psychological needs as well. If the so-called "secondary gains" of the illness have not been adequately replaced, the symptoms will come back.

Hermes overcame Argus, the monster with a thousand eyes, by putting him to sleep with music before slaying him. Faced with a client who is destroying himself, the therapist is also in mortal combat with a thousand-eyed monster. If the ulcer is taken care of, it's the headache that carries on the destruction; if the headache is relieved, a dislocated vertebra may be next. The monster, like Argus, always has one more eye. The patient, of course, must be willing to fight and put his whole soul into it, but the therapist is also fully engaged. To defeat Argus, both must be extremely vigilant and seize the one moment when the monster may be overcome.

An alert therapist must also be capable of recognizing the lie in a patient, perhaps in the form of defensiveness or unconscious withdrawal, as if Argus was only pretending to be asleep or wasn't sleeping with all his eyes. Let's not forget that Hermes as patron of liars suggests that a therapist is also at fault if he thinks his patients never lie to him. A therapist without metis has trouble detecting a symptom's disguises, the lies hidden behind the defense mechanisms. Hermes used a diversion to kill the monster; he put him to sleep with his flute-playing. Doesn't the therapist do the same with a patient whose problem is psychosomatic? He puts the problem to sleep (lowering defense mechanisms) in order to root it out; he charms the monster in order to kill it. This is one of Hermes' favorite tactics, avoiding any direct attack but vanquishing Argus nevertheless. Today we need him more than ever, because psychological pain in its many disguises has become an enormous monster that eats away at our very substance. Scientific medicine is of no use in the treatment of these Argus pains.

Legend says that Hermes first acquired the caduceus from the hands of Apollo in exchange for the lyre that Hermes had just invented. But the caduceus changes hands more than once. At the moment when Apollo became the most glorious figure of the scientific spirit, the caduceus reappeared in the hands of his son Asclepius. His appearance marks the beginning of opposition to Hermes-style medicine although, when Asclepius came into the world, myth tells us that it is Hermes who saved him from death.

The medicine practiced by Asclepius formed the bridge between the ancient practices of healers and magicians and the new scientific medicine under the sign of Apollo and his son. This passage from Hermes to Apollo marks the secularization of medicine. The new medical schools and physicians' groups kept their distance from the healers and priests in the temples. The doctors who swore an oath to Apollo scorned the practices of shamanistic medicine despite an impressive record of success. At Cnide, physicians began making more and more precise observations, firmly putting aside the rituals and philosophical theories about health which flourished around them. They perfected as never before the practice of careful observation, a discipline considered today to be the first step in any scientific undertaking. They used a language full of images and analogies to transmit their results. Thus, to describe a certain kind of consumption, the observer notes that the patient made whistling sounds "as if speaking through a reed"; a patient with a different lung disease is observed as "opening his nostrils like a galloping horse with his tongue hanging out like a parched dog in the summer heat." The Cnideans were content to observe and to write vividly about their observations. They declined to develop theories or to systematize their observations in any way.

Another school at Cos, where Hippocrates was master, moved scientific inquiry up a notch. Hippocrates, the Greek medical genius incarnate, adopted the observational method of the Cnideans and proposed that reason and the direct experience of the five senses be applied to the study of illness. Under the influence of these two great schools of Cnide and Cos, possession, sorcery and magic dropped out as causes of illness and Greek rationalism took the upper hand. Hippocrates expressed the spirit of his time when he stated apropos of epilepsy: "Some people believe it's a question of divine intervention. That's wrong. It's a natural illness whose cause we do not yet understand."

At Cos physicians went beyond observation to develop inductive scientific explanations of observed facts; they thus worked on concepts. Their medical theories, reworked in time by Galen, remained in force into the seventeenth century. This faith in science replaced the religious faith that gave priests and priestesses their power to heal. There were fewer and fewer "miraculous" healings in Greece as doctors replaced healers. They began to practice their art in a scientific spirit even before the word *science* took on the meaning we give it today. Women were excluded from the medical profession, and "old wives' remedies" were seen as retrogressive.

But the caduceus, even if in the hands of the sons of Apollo, nonetheless still symbolized the holistic side of Hippocratic medicine. In fact, even though the medical groups were hostile toward temple healers, they admitted that a true doctor must pay attention to a patient's psychological life. They didn't try to separate the person into body and spirit, and they took into consideration the patient's psychological and social milieu. In their eyes the practice of medicine required both knowledge and wisdom, and it became an elevated cultural form. Nevertheless, the passing of the caduceus to Apollo Alexicos (i.e., he who pursues illness)—a solar God and a personification of daylight consciousness, of reason, and of scientific inquiry—marks the end of shamanistic medicine in Western culture.

The development of science and its application to medicine are certainly worth our taking pride in. All the more reason why we must be concerned about any regression or breach of scientific rigor. When a doctor short-circuits the scientific process by passing directly from symptom to remedy, for example, he regresses to the pre-scientific method of trial and error. The doctor who brings out his prescription pad the moment one sits down and then says "come back and see me in a week if it's not better" (meaning, we'll try something else) could well be back at Cnide and Cos.

With the so-called "alternative" therapies of today, regression occurs whenever charms and amulets—like crystals and mini-pyramids—are offered under a pseudo-scientific guise. This phenomenon reveals a confusion between two archetypes, Hermes and Apollo, and the two types of medicine they represent, so that the patient no longer knows what he's dealing with—a witch doctor or a scientist? And the confusion is on both sides: some doctors, in the mistaken belief that it's easy to bring about change in another person, move into the sorcerer's role without being aware of it. I know some doctors who believe that a half hour's exhortation about avoiding stress, under pain of death from cardiac arrest, will be enough to persuade the patient to change his life, to restructure his personality.

A young woman recently reported to me a rather extreme example of the psychological naïveté of physicians. Her father, age fifty-five, is a tense man who has always found it difficult to relax. After his first cardiac episode he consulted a cardiologist who responded as follows: "Sir, I've studied your test results, and I can say to you clearly that if you don't relax you'll be dead in five years." This warning is completely absurd, even if based on reasonable scientific prediction. First of all, if the patient has a heart problem it's because he doesn't know how to relax; secondly, the "relax or die" threat raises his tension to a dangerous level and aggravates the problem instead of leading to a solution. In fact the cardiologist instilled such fear in his patient that he had a second attack that very night.

All of Hermes' metis was needed in this case. To teach someone to relax is not the proper sphere of Apollo, but it falls well within the capabilities of Hermes. His place in medicine is even more crucial today in view of the fact that psychosomatic troubles increase in direct proportion to society's ability to provide itself with a sophisticated scientific medical system. Medicine has a twofold task to accomplish and two archetypes to acknowledge. There's medical research, but also there's a resurgence of treatments that were effective in the temples—baths, dances, rituals, massage, fasts, pilgrimages, an understanding of the body–soul connection, and above all the restoration of intuitive communication (metis) between therapist and client.

The present confusion between scientific and holistic medicines has a positive side. We can see the confusion as the beginnings of a merging, a system that will produce a more complete balance. We certainly need a medicine which can once again be symbolized by the caduceus. Who would want a holistic approach that couldn't keep up with scientific advances? There's no need to die of peritonitis trying to prove the curative power of herbal tea. On the other hand, translating all of our ills into clinical terms has reached a point of absurdity. In many cases science itself acknowledges its inability to deal with the complexity of the soul–body connection because the soul half cannot be studied in the laboratory. Besides there is more than one half affecting health. We now have a medical field called psycho-neuro-immunology (PNI), to which we will surely soon be adding eco-socio-psycho-neuro-immunology. To grasp that connection one needs a talent for communication instead of a microscope.

Today, a large proportion of medical decisions flow from a body of scientific knowledge that is so systematized that a computer can take over part of the physician's job. Even if he doesn't use a computer, the doctor who treats a patient every five minutes has been programmed. The input consists of compiling a list of symptoms and a medical history, then adding the results of laboratory tests. Medical theory, perfected over the centuries since Cos, enables him to come up with a diagnosis, treatment and prognosis. Whether the patient spends three minutes or three hours with such a doctor is not very important; if he can arrive at a correct readout in three minutes, why prolong the consultation? Here there's no need for Hermes' intuition, only a rigorous logic based on the most recent results of scientific investigation and statistics. Even if the doctor takes the trouble to ask what's bothering you and why you're so tense, it carries no weight if the reply to the question has no effect on the program as it unfolds.

The defensive attitude of doctors toward new computer capabilities is revealing. They have disqualified their holistic rivals for a long time by citing their weak scientific basis. What will these doctors say when they see themselves outflanked by expert systems which are even more informed and more scientifically rigorous than themselves? A clue to their reaction can be seen in an editorial by Dr. Barnett entitled "The Computer and Clinical Judgment," published in 1982 in the prestigious *New England Journal of Medicine*. He begins by reassuring his readers:

> The optimistic expectation of 20 years ago that computer technology would also come to play an important part in clinical decisions has not been realized, and there are few if any situations in which computers are being routinely used to assist in either medical diagnosis or the choice of therapy. . . .[38]

What he says is true, but it conceals an important fact—the opposition of doctors and medical associations who feel threatened, and justifiably so, by the eventual widespread use of computer systems. Since the publication of this editorial these systems have significantly improved, even though their use has not proliferated. It therefore seems reasonable to predict that this expertise will not go unused for long, especially since the companies investing in the production of software are not necessarily controlled by the medical community. Predictably, these companies will find buyers. Dr. Barnett's argument becomes very interesting when he adds:

> In the real world it is necessary that the doctor not only understand the statistical relations of signs and symptoms to the various possible diseases but also have the wisdom and common sense that derive from the understanding and experience of everyday human existence. It is this last requirement that represents the greatest weakness (and perhaps the ultimate limitation) of computer technology in dealing in any comprehensive fashion with the problem of clinical diagnosis.

It's understandable that he would insist on wisdom, common sense, etc., to differentiate between the practitioner and the computer. But where will doctors go to find that wisdom? The Hermes part of medicine is precisely what the holistic movement has tried to resurrect, the part that Apollonian medicine has scorned since the death of Hippocrates. Which of the two will go find the other? Is it simpler to inject some wisdom into a robot-doctor, or would it be more efficient to put the true robots, the expert systems, the laboratories and the public funds at the disposition of those who have already developed a holistic concept of health in their practices, who have already acquired a level of wisdom? In short, who has the better chance of developing a complete view of the individual patient; who will deserve to carry the caduceus? This confrontation cannot be avoided, because soon computer-aided diagnostic tools and laboratory services will outperform the ordinary doctor in terms of scientific accuracy, and he will have to develop an expertise of his own that does not compete with the computer. The contest will be, in the end, on these grounds.

We need both Apollo and Hermes, that is, a medicine that is

impeccable on the scientific level yet skillful in helping the patient
not to turn on himself when his soul is in pain and his demons attack him. Healers, temple priests and priestesses, and later the
physicians of the great Hippocratic schools were always endowed
with mythological attributes which gave them a halo of power.
This has transferred to the modern doctor, who enjoys a level
of social and financial recognition that is staunchly protected.
Doctors lay claim to a professional and social identity and all
the material advantages that ensue, as well as to a mythic identity which authorizes them to see themselves as heroes, masters,
saviors.

But in pre-scientific medicine, if the priest had a right to his own
myth the patient had a right to his, too. The patient had embarked
on a quest, a pilgrimage; he prepared himself for an encounter
with a divinity and participated in the healing process with all his
soul. The priest or priestess acted as guide, but it was the patient's
responsibility to come face to face with the divinity. This relationship is analogous to the one that exists today between client and
therapist. The therapist sets the conditions, performs the ritual,
and guides the client, who is in fact the true hero of this adventure.

As modern medicine progressed, the patient lost his myth and
the doctor benefited from that loss. The sick person no longer
counts at all in the eyes of official medicine; he is just barely a body
and in many cases just part of a body. He has lost the dignity that
used to accompany suffering. (I won't even mention here the
humiliation of being treated like a stupid child or a hysterical embarrassment, an experience almost all women have encountered at
least once in their lives in the gynecologist's office or the delivery
room.) In this mythic combat with illness it's the doctor who is the
hero, whereas the patient has become banal, anonymous, without
mythological attributes. He doesn't speak, he is an object under
treatment. Nameless and without feeling, he might as well be a
laboratory animal. He is both dazzled by medical power and de-
mythified in his own being.

Much has been said about the holistic nature of alternative
medicine, as distinct from official medicine, but the emergence of a
new myth for the patient is crucial for the future of mercurial
medicine. The patient must reclaim his own archetypal dimension
if he is to participate fully in this fight for survival and health.
Hermes, God of travelers, adventurers, pilgrims, and all those

who take to the road in search of spiritual revelation, pushes us to change our lives, our values, our diet, and to explore new territory, including the "final voyage" during which he serves as "guide of souls."

The caduceus may pass from one hand to another, from official medicine to holistic medicine, but in a polytheistic world no one divinity can possess the whole truth, and each must acknowledge the necessary contribution of the other.

The Magician

Mythic thought and scientific thought have at least one attribute in common: the discovery of connections between things, beings and situations which don't appear to be linked. But science moves from the general to the particular through a deductive linear process, whereas myth does the opposite. It connects the particular to a larger "gestalt," tracing the connection between a small isolated event and global consciousness, between an individual act and its archetypal component. Since this assumes a much larger perspective, it means learning to follow several paths at once. Apollo leads us on the linear roads (or highways, perhaps) of science, while Hermes is the guide into the complex network of symbolic relationships. To learn more about Hermes-magician, we'll consider first the Hermes that seems fascinated with a specific form of magic: binding and unbinding, tying and untying, attaching and detaching.

It's easy to make a psychological connection between emotional situations and words like weaving, knotting, braiding, twisting, binding. The sorcerer, the therapist, the shaman and the healer are all caught up in a form of magic in which Hermes appears, making and unmaking emotional connections, tying and untying psychological knots. Apollo tries to tie up Hermes-the-thief, but here is what happens:

> He [Apollo] spoke,
> and started tying up
> the arms of the god
> with powerful thongs of willow.
> Those he put on his feet, however,

suddenly started growing
down into the ground,
twisting together,
and easily tangled up
all the wild cattle there—
thanks to the schemes
of tricky Hermes.
Apollo was shocked![39]

Then looking "up and down, suggestively, a fire twinkling in his eyes," Hermes brings out his lyre and enchants Apollo with his music. The initial situation is now reversed. Not only are Apollo's cattle tangled up with thongs of willow, but Apollo himself is emotionally "attached" to Hermes.

There are at least three levels of meaning to Hermes' gift of binding and unbinding. First of all, Hermes is literally the God of keys and doors, of fishing nets and fishhooks. It was Hermes who freed Ares, the God of war, when he was bound in chains: "Borne unto Hermes tidings, and he it was stole away Ares, far outworn already...."[40]

Secondly, language itself reflects a symbolic level of meaning in many expressions about binding: one is "bound" by a promise, "hooked" by love, "attached" to a child, "held back" by fear, or one's attention is "riveted" on something important. Our mother is a primary "attachment," death is our "undoing," we "tie the knot" when we marry, we "break up" when we divorce. Like the Sirens who held Ulysses under the spell of their song, Hermes can hold, hypnotize, and put to sleep as well as untie, wake up, and break the bonds.[41]

Seduction is a third shade of meaning. Seduction has a magical element to it, a special tie holding one person to another. Hermes has some of Aphrodite's qualities but in a masculine mode. Developing these qualities leads of course to charisma and charm.[42] But the seductive power of Hermes has a double edge, as do all seductions and all powers. In addition to attraction, exchange, contentment and the happiness of the one seduced, there is a fraudulent element, if only the realization that what seemed eternal certainly is not! In love affairs, Hermes, Eros and Aphrodite form an irresistible trio. If Aphrodite seduces in all possible ways,

Hermes is especially gifted in the use of words, and both he and Eros are "whisperers" whose murmurings cast an enveloping spell.

> Seduction is so much due to words! Grand avowals, false oaths, lies, deceptions, excuses, Hermes is never at a loss for finds and does everything with equal conviction! Interpreter to foreigners, truce-bearer to combatants, he changes neither his nature nor his role when he acts as go-between to lovers.[43]

Whether it be stolen love (adultery) or negotiated love (marriage), Hermes and Aphrodite weave a bond of mutual attraction between two people. Hermes *prohegetes* supports marriage in two ways: he whispers to the young wife the words which will seduce her husband, and he oversees the practice of exogamy, the wife leaving one clan for another.

Hermes shares with Aphrodite and Demeter the honor of being invoked when fertility is at stake, either with couples or with flocks and herds. In spite of his feminine intelligence Hermes, like Dionysos, is also represented as a ram. Intensity of sexual emotion, however, is not Hermes' business; that belongs to Dionysos and Aphrodite. His business is getting this libido into circulation. Some men powerfully endowed with Dionysian energy but deprived of mercurial seduction may appear to their feminine partners like raging beasts, overcome with urgent and primitive sexual needs. Women who see the love-game as an exchange of subtle messages (not a meal for the starving) are repelled by their style. Hermes could teach them how to make contact with the desired partner, seduce her, and gain reciprocal satisfaction through what is aptly called in French "*le commerce amoureux.*" In this kind of business, the more exchange there is, the more there is to exchange! Hermes presides over the fecundity of money (as God of commerce), of flocks and herds (the ram), and of couples (*prohegetes*). In Greek the word *tocos* means both capital and the increase of a flock through its fertility. Wealth then, in Hermes' terms, is essentially a question of fertility, communication and exchange.

On the psychological level, people who haven't given enough attention to Hermes generally find it hard to give of themselves, to be involved, to seduce, or be seduced. These people hold back, build up reserves, rein in their sexual, affective and intellectual energy, even when it is considerable. They may be well-endowed, generous and fecund, but lack the artfulness and intuition in the practice of the business of love—and don't we call love "an affair"?

The binding power of Hermes allows lovers to communicate, to contract a marriage. As the lovers undo their buttons and belts, they bind more intimately with each other. Undressing as in Salome and the Dance of Veils is of course an Aphroditic seduction, but it is also a Hermetic disclosure of secrets. The bikini, the snap and the zipper are fine for the big-bang theory of sexuality, but they leave out Hermes and Aphrodite.

As the overseer of binding and unbinding, Hermes has a special symbolic role at the moment of birth, that is, the moment of cutting the umbilical cord. In Greek the word for being pregnant can be rendered as "being bound" and that for childbirth as "being unbound." At the moment of birth the Greek women undid all cords, belts and buckles and opened all doors, locks and coffers. The symbolism of cutting the cord, of severing a bond, is so obvious at the moment of childbirth that it takes a society as distressed in its symbolic life as ours not to see how odious it is to restrain or, more precisely, to handcuff a woman in labor. Not only that, she is asked to keep her voice down and her emotions in check! This medical barbarity not only disrupts the birth process but the whole symbolic function as well: how can a woman allow a child to be born, grow up and detach itself when she herself is bound and gagged? How can she not become frigid when the immense release of sexual and emotional energy at childbirth is treated as unacceptable? Where in the world is Hermes, opener of doors and bodies?

The most difficult phase of childbirth is always the passage through the neck of the uterus; it's the moment when the gate to life must open. The woman can't push yet. She must open herself and open again so that the child may pass through, and it is then that she begins to tremble with all her being. This moment belongs to Artemis in its wildness and to Hermes. Everything that closes up prolongs suffering and turns into a tortured experience what could be a grand moment of initiation for a woman. Distrust, rudeness, noise, fear, the arrogance of obstetricians, their pleasure in dominating the woman, in dominating the other man, the father—in short, all that characterizes obstetrics in the twentieth century is contrary to the magic of Hermes who, along with Illythia and

Artemis, the Goddesses of childbirth, possesses the power to un-
bind. Forceps powerfully epitomize anti-Hermes medicine. Birth is
not only a physical event; it is also an extremely intense emotional
experience which exacerbates any psychological conflicts that may
exist. One may become aware of one's most difficult inner knots
and has to untie them in a supreme effort. No forceps will do that.
If Hermes is given a chance, he can not only untie the umbilical
cord but many other and older problem knots that pull from all
sides during childbirth.

Hermes, whom Jung considered the archetype of the unconscious, is naturally present at such a time, along with Illythia,
Demeter, Artemis and Dionysos. In fact the whole Greek pantheon
seems to want to share this crucial moment of existence. All the
Gods and Goddesses are associated in one way or another with the
birth event. A successful birth not only produces a healthy child
but also represents a profound psychological denouement for the
woman, the man, and the couple, because it's the perfect moment
for change to take place. When a child is born, what was will never
again be the same.

Transitions

The metal associated with Hermes is mercury. The alchemists
called it quicksilver or liquid silver because of its liveliness, its
malleability and its capacity to transform itself. They recognized it
as the prime element in all transformations, even though a second
element (needed to make the transformation stick) does not belong
to Hermes.

> He stands at the boundaries of premises, cross-roads, gates of
> towns, and houses, locks, limits of properties, and happens wher-
> ever change occurs: *strophaïos*, he slews round not only doors upon
> hinges but also man upon this very line of division, helping him
> to swing from within to without.[44]

Hermes transforms himself endlessly, for his nature is as change-
able and unstable as the metal he represents. At a temperature
where other metals are hard, mercury is liquid and flowing. Hermes, more than any other God, changes location (God of travel),

changes form (polymorphism), changes the truth (sophist), changes his price (merchant), keeps a discussion moving (herald). An archetype standing for change itself, he pops up whenever change is imminent: being born, growing up, going on a trip, getting married, falling asleep (Hermes *hypnodotes*, giver of sleep) and, finally, dying, the great mutation overseen by Hermes psychopomp. The mercurial element within a personality brings mobility and unpredictability. The constant shimmering of mercurial energy is very seductive in those who possess it, a fascination equaled only by Aphrodite's special brand of attraction. Are we not all fascinated by mercury? It's fun to try to hold it in your hand; it flees at the tiniest motion. Mercurial personalities are difficult to grasp and impossible to restrain. The ease with which mercury joins other metals recalls Hermes' psychological capacity to establish relationships and make friends, which makes him a communications genius.

In its ordinary state mercury is both a metal and a liquid, and, as we've seen, Hermes is bivalent—both order and chaos, truth and falsehood, the mediator between life and death, between celestial values and terrestrial values (Hermes Uranos and Hermes Chthonian). He refuses to stay put; he wants to be open on all sides. This quality of openness is a gift that the puer brings with him. James Hillman and his collaborators in *Puer Papers* have helped to rehabilitate this archetype, exploring the psychology of puer for whom the image of the open door is fundamental. The characteristic traits of the puer—untidiness, exhibitionism, forgetfulness and tardiness, not keeping to schedule, various distractions and escapes which could come under the heading of a "weak ego," and even the problems and hurts that result from this behavior—all are also doors or cracks through which the spirit may enter.[45]

Mercury represents the mobile, volatile element in any transformation. But according to alchemical theory, the presence of a second element called "the fixed" is needed for change to be actualized. This image reminds us that the principle of change (Hermes) alone is not enough for change to take place but must be joined to its opposite, fixedness (Hestia). To illustrate this process, let's take the example of dyeing cloth, a subject dear to alchemists. The mercurial element is the new color, but if the mixture doesn't contain the fixative, the change will not last and the old color will reappear when water (time) flows over the material. Here alchemy joins with psychology, which acknowledges in all personality changes a first step where it seems easy to break with old behavior patterns, to shake off a neurosis and let puer take over. It's fun to break up everything and thumb one's nose at senex responsibilities. Quick cures ("change your life in four sessions") specialize in this first phase of personal change.

But if the effort ends with this visit from Hermes the new state will not become established, and then one of two things happens: either the person is back at square one, change having disappeared after the first washing, as with a dye of poor quality, or else there is constant change and Hermes begins to manifest as ongoing disruption and disorder. Then every possible color shows up: every morning there's a new beginning, starting from scratch, new job, new friends, new clothes, new apartment—never getting a hold on a lasting identity. In its extreme form this may lead to vagrancy: empty hands, empty pockets, don't ask me to stay in one place! Those who have money are protected from the status of streetbum, but they still seem like scatterbrained overgrown children, redecorating their houses with each fad, looking for a new network of relations with each step up the social ladder.

Psychologists not only encounter this problem but also sometimes contribute to it: some clients consume every therapy in the marketplace. They spend their entire adult lives in one form of therapy or another, whatever is in fashion, and yet seem impervious to any real change. Therapies are shaken off like water off a duck's back. This problem persists with the client's enjoyment of his puer instability, while the therapist gets stuck in a senex posture. It may be useful, as López-Pedraza suggests, for the therapist to move in Hermes' direction: the client's attraction by the senex pole thereby establishes a balance.[46] Perhaps the analyst needs to have an interesting life himself, so that the client can stop playing the child prodigy bombarded with fascinating dreams, overwhelmed with complex emotions, recounting a life full of sudden new developments (real or imaginary), all of which are apt to attract an analyst whose life is monotonous.

The personality with no Hermetic qualities lacks suppleness and adaptability. The personality with exclusively Hermetic qualities may lose his way as he tries to navigate through many escapades, detours and evasions. When it gets to the point where one can't see the forest for the trees, somewhere a puer–senex polarization has become entrenched.

The mercurial quality produces people who seem to slip through one's fingers and transform themselves repeatedly. Of course, this is an excellent defense against domination and control from the outside; one can't control something one can't get a grip on. Hermes avoids confrontation with any Zeus through his roguish behavior. But this incessant flight can lead to problems and impasses unresolvable by a simple about-face. As is true of all archetypes, Hermes has his own pathology. In schizoid pathology, the capacity for integration no longer functions, the wheel of change turns endlessly, the compass needle no longer points North. Schizoid withdrawal can be seen as a retreat from the unbearable contradictions that the spirit of Hermes can no longer overcome. Some schizoid personalities can sense the lies and evasions of people around them. They have an affinity for the world of symbols and myths and a natural tendency to speak on several levels at once. But, cruelly, they lack the ability to transform their intuitions into a communicable form. Rather than serving human relationships, their intuition tends to foster paranoia.

To deal with the second principle of change—called fixation by alchemy, integration by humanistic psychology, recrystallization of attitudes by social psychology, and centration by Orientalist psychology—we must move on to what archetypal psychology labels the senex archetype. We must go toward father Zeus and old Saturn and, also, on another level, toward Hestia. She is the Goddess who chooses stability over change, who welcomes the adventurer into her house and feeds him well on the condition that he wipe his boots on the doormat before stepping on her shining kitchen floor, into her peaceful domestic realm. She offers focus (foyer or hearth) to the volatile dispersion of Hermes–Puer.

Is There a Need to Conceal?

Hermes made a deal with the God Hades, guardian of the dead. He would lead souls to their final resting place and keep the register of the dead, and in return Hades would lend him the cap of invisibility. At the end of the pagan world Hermes' spirit took refuge in the esoteric, reappearing in the legendary alchemist of the Middle Ages, the imposing Hermes Trismegistus, a far cry from the divine rogue of the Greeks.

It isn't necessary to belong to an esoteric sect to understand that some states of consciousness naturally tend to be surrounded by mystery: this is in part because they elude verbal explanations. The famous secrets of esoteric groups are not so much secrets as rituals by which the uninitiated are brought to a certain level of consciousness whereby they can now understand something hitherto unavailable to their awareness. Most of the time the secret is nothing other than the ability to see what is already there, which is the goal of the initiation.

In this sense humor is often esoteric. Comical situations that arise within one group of people aren't funny when told to others. Even if you try to explain exactly why something is funny, you can't get more than a smile from the outsider. Usually you end up saying "I guess you had to be there," which is like saying "you're not an initiate; everything has been explained and you still can't understand." Embracing a worldview that involves "revelation" and speaking a "hermetic" language are ways of donning the cap that allows us to see without being seen. Furthermore, the esoteric arises whenever something needs to be hidden from society or when some group intimacy needs to be protected. The esoteric is part of the Hermes archetype and part of communication in general. Every time there's a "we" and a "they," the group generates a secret aura around itself and the secrecy increases as the group life intensifies. The esoteric in Hermes has to do with the way mythic thought functions: it is either grasped immediately and fully or not at all. It is a revelation.

Even though the esoteric is frequently expressed in groups through secret rituals, it is essentially a personal experience, not a joining with others in a collective *belief* or doctrine. Belief is the opposite of revelation. Hermes' experiential wisdom is nocturnal and feminine, the intuition of Metis. The daylight knowledge of Apollo, provided by direct evidence and expressed in unequivocal terms, cannot account for it; one has to go through the experience.

All the Gods and Goddesses lend themselves to caricature. Each can become inflated and claim to occupy the entire divine ground, something like the globally applied theories that purport to explain everything—Freud, for example, or Marx, or Hermes Trisme-

gistus, the Thrice-Great Alchemist of the Middle Ages. This
Hermes is eager to incorporate everything in himself. As Thrice-
Great he has another pair of wings at the base of the caduceus,
indicating that he has everything: the principle of fixation as well
as volatility. But this synthesis into one figure forgets the in-
terdependence of polytheism, which assumes that each God and
Goddess expresses an area of weakness as well as an area of
strength, a limitation that can only be overcome by a close—one
might almost say ecological—connection to other divinities. Hermes Trismegistus appropriates to himself what he lacks, the fixed
principle, just as Zeus, when he became God-the-Father, swallowed his wife so as to become both father and mother! Apollo,
too, tempted by this monotheistic bulimia, claims to explain
everything by science alone, calling moonlight darkness, while
Dionysos, having become the God Orpheus, had to be the sole
source of knowledge and ecstasy to his devotees.

Hermes Trismegistus is considered to be the founder of esoteric
astrology and alchemy. With him alchemy, already incomprehen-
sible to the uninitiated, became even more enigmatic and impenetrable, imitating and maybe influenced by the dogmatic faith
of Christianity. The sacred texts were said to have been revealed
by Hermes and gathered into several volumes, the alchemical
Bible.

The meaning usually given to the word *hermetic*—that is,
closed, sealed off (like a hermetically sealed jar that allows no air
to enter or escape), understood only by the initiated—no longer
seems quite appropriate for the divine rogue who was so popular
and available and open to the Greeks. Hermes Trismegistus, for
that matter, owes more to the senex than to the Greek Hermes,
and the popularity of esoteric alchemy today owes more to an inflated spirit of Hermes Trismegistus than to the young and playful
Hermes of the agora.[47] There is some absurdity in a conception of
alchemy understood as a process of *hiding* since the alchemist's
task is precisely the opposite: it is not to *hide* a secret process but
to *reveal* it. A very good teacher, one who has the ability to help us
understand complex matters, is more of an alchemist than an
esoteric freak knowledgeable in the history of alchemical symbols.
Let us not forget that Hermes is, after all, God of *communication*,
not a God of uncommunicability.

In that context of strict acceptance, *spiritual alchemy* is equally absurd from a Hermetic perspective: how is it possible for alchemy to be exclusively "spiritual" when its primary concern is with matter? Alchemy is precisely about the interpenetration of the material and spiritual realms.

Sylvain Matton who writes the introduction to the reprint of the alchemical writings of Dom Pernety, first published in Paris in 1758,[48] demonstrates how the mythological stories are, in Dom Pernety's book, explicitly given while the chemical processes are being turned into metaphors. Myth is all clear; chemistry is obscure. It is often believed that the treatises on alchemy, with their frequent references to the chemistry of physical substances, should be understood on a different level as treatises on soul processes. But, as Sylvain Matton argues, it may well be that mythographic literature hides a treatise on chemistry instead of alchemy's hiding a treatise on psychology.

Whatever the hidden meaning, alchemical knowledge couldn't be communicated neatly and directly like modern chemistry; it was closer to the multi-level meanings of myth. A myth can hide a chemical formula or a political struggle, a historical fact, a psychological complex, an economic struggle, an ecological wisdom, a feminist protest, an intellectual insight. As was true of the Eleusinian mysteries, words are often not enough to account for certain subtle realities; symbolic communication is more appropriate—even, one could argue, more precise since it accounts for subtleties that words cannot convey.

Did alchemy keep alive the spirit of Hermes? I do not know, but I do know that I prefer Hermes the Thief, the Trickster, Guide of Souls, and God of Communications to the Thrice-Great Hermes.

> Hail to you,
> son of Zeus and Maia.
> I began this hymn
> for you
> and now I will pass on
> to another hymn.
> Farewell,
> dispenser of favors,
> guide,
> giver of good things.[49]

PART THREE

Goddess Memory

Why was my grandfather called "the bear," and why was I given my aunt's first name? Who planted the yellow flowers around my childhood home? Why was my mother so happy there? I'd like so much for her to tell me what I was like as a child. If no one can answer my questions, I'll invent a plausible response, blending Memory and Imagination, as in the Renaissance. I need those memories because they carry my identity. Without the Goddess Memory the myth in which I live dissolves. The symbols seem less intimate: the bear, the yellow flowers, the house on the mountain don't evoke anything special, and the images lose their resonance. One can see why the ancient Greeks personified Mnemosyne as one of the Titanesses, those gigantic Goddesses of creation, for she is at the source of every culture and her work is essential to the survival of every group.

The concept of memory conceals such different realities that it is useful to provide a few intellectual bench marks. In an oral culture memory includes all knowledge, all practical know-how, all history, and all the mythology handed down from one generation to another. The ancient Greeks made a Goddess of that sort of Memory—Mnemosyne. Today the same word—*memory*—describes my ability to memorize the multiplication tables, the power of a computer, and the way I remember my grandmother. Therefore, in order to understand clearly what Memory (with a capital letter) stands for, we must separate her from the all-inclusive meaning of the word *memory*.

Nowadays, we tend to think it's enough to create museums and libraries to fulfill the function of Memory. We maintain archives, train historians, and encourage groups to preserve their common heritage and invest in computers with enormous memory banks. Of course these are all necessary, but literacy—and, even more, computer literacy—can make us all victims of amnesia. It is commonplace to say that literacy has made us lose our mnemonic ability: since writing serves as a memory-aid, it is no longer necessary to develop the ability to remember as in an oral culture.

It is understandable why the "art of memory" fell into disuse.[1] Who can repeat the names of two thousand people in the order in which they are presented, as Seneca, professor of rhetoric, could do? Before a class of two hundred students, each reciting a verse of poetry, he could repeat each verse as given beginning with the last. But however impressive such mnemonic ability, we must not reduce memory to it. Neither should we restrict her territory to history books, to chronicles, archives or data banks. Much more than all that, she is after all a Titaness, a cosmic element.

Some believe that our respect for human memory can be restored by pointing out that the best computers can store a billion bits of information, whereas, according to neurobiologists, human memory is capable of storing 100 trillion bits of information. But to measure Memory against the criteria for computer-memory only heightens the confusion between Memory, mother of the Muses, and the computer-memory, child of Apollo and Hephaestos. Just as a professor correcting a student paper is justified in judging the breadth of a work by the number of pages written, the impressive capacity for retention of human memory deserves our admiration. We are in fact able to retain a lot of facts. But to judge memory by this one quantitative measure would be like judging the value of a thesis according to the weight of the manuscript. The emergence of a culture in which computers provide the most popular metaphor for imagining human memory invites another look at Mnemosyne, for this Goddess is so clearly the opposite of computer-memory that she could well be the ideal counterweight to the computer culture.

Most philosophical textbooks and manuals on the subject of memory go back (a) to Plato and his theory of memory, according to which all knowledge is merely reminiscence; (b) to Aristotle, according to whom Memory is "the having of an regarded as a copy of that of which it is an image;"[2] or (c) to the distinctions established by Henri Bergson, according to which the memory of procedures (such as how to ride a bicycle proceeds from a different kind of memory than the collection of personal history. Since these philosophical distinctions are well-known, we won't discuss them further here.[3] Rather, let's try to get hold of Mnemosyne as she relates, first of all, to our collective past (oral culture), secondly to the present (literate culture), and last in terms of the future (computer-literate culture).

Scientific culture has led us to consider memory from a utilitarian point of view and to value it somewhere below intelligence. This overlooks the fact that Memory was a Goddess before the supremacy of science and Apollo, a Goddess whose voice we can still hear.

Oral Memory: The Voice of Mnemosyne

Mnemosyne uses the structures of narrative, epic, song or myth to preserve remembrance. She loves repetition, rhyme, rhythms and the strong images that hold narrative together. Naturally linked to a subjective idea of memory and to mythical thought, she doesn't worry much about facts and dates, nor about their linear or causal sequence. Her goal is to evoke rather than to describe. In this style of memory the factual and the symbolic, the historical and the mythical, "real" events and "imaginary" happenings are all tangled up inextricably. The memory at work in oral cultures allows for modification and adjustment, sometimes reversing the meaning of an event. It's an active memory which breaks into consciousness through archetypes, dreams and myths, fantasies, symbols and artistic work. It selects and organizes the past, putting into context what is recollected. Sometimes it pays close attention to what was intensely lived, while at other times it selects events which seem unimportant but are endowed with a depth that can neither be denied nor explained.

Mnemosyne is a voice, the voice of an oral culture, a female voice, a soul voice. It can come in the night as a dream, in a car as a project or longing, in bed with a lover as a sudden recollection. But it is not just of the past, a taped recording; it is constructive, evocative, poignant, and the beginning of musing as Mnemosyne was the mother of the Muses. To look for a piece of information in this context means to seek out the person (the voice) that can tell me the story that includes that information. Expressions like "to search one's memory" or "to erase from memory" only make sense in a literate culture, because in an oral culture memory is nowhere metaphorically in-scribed. Rather, it speaks out. Scientists who study memory have long focused their research on the brain, acknowledged as the organ of memory. The Greeks, however, placed the seat of memory in the heart (they considered the brain

to be a blood-cooling mechanism, a little like an automobile ra-
diator). Metaphorically, they thought of Memory as the voice of a
Goddess, whereas our favorite metaphors have been first of all the
book, the dictionary, then the computer. These metaphors make
memory a passive tool[4] of the ego which draws what it needs from
the brain, like a scholar going to his library shelves or a program-
mer accessing information from a disk.

Psychotherapists resist both metaphors, the library-memory and
the computer-memory. Since Freud we've allowed ourselves to act
as if memories can be imprinted, not just in the brain, but in the
whole body, in a paralyzed arm which refuses to budge, in a back
which bends as if weighed down. Wilhelm Reich's approach[5] or
Alexander Lowen's bioenergetics[6] are extreme examples of a conception of memory in which the brain does not play a central role.
The therapist acts as if, for example, the memory of a sorrow
could spring up again by his massaging the throat muscles whose
contraction prevents the tears from flowing, as if the throat itself
kept the memory.

Artists also work with a fantasy of memory imprinted in the
body rather than localized in the brain. The artist works with
Mnemosyne and her daughters, the Muses; he needs an event, a
tale, an emotion, a sensation for the remembrance to emerge.
Marcel Proust, a true son of Mnemosyne's, knows the importance
of the five senses to reconstruct the "vast structure of recollection."

> But when from the long-distant past nothing subsists, after the
> people are dead, after the things are broken and scattered, taste
> and smell alone, more fragile but more enduring, more unsub-
> stantial, more persistent, more faithful, remain poised a long time,
> like souls, remembering, waiting, hoping, amid the ruins of all the
> rest; and bear unflinchingly, in the tiny and almost impalpable drop
> of their essence, the vast structure of recollection.[7]

In our daily experience we also sense that "the body remembers"; it's the body that remembers the taste of cherries or the
aroma of a warm strawberry tart in June. Research in neurology
and molecular biochemistry can help us map the circuits of memory. Science can tell us that the aroma of the strawberry tart
passes through the olfactory nerve, which moves the information
to the hippocampus, which adds its "emotional equivalent" to the

experience. For example, a coloration of happiness might be added to the memory of those strawberry pies that I take the time to bake, sometimes, at the summer house in June. Once past the hippocampus, the olfactory memory resides in the cerebral cortex at a site corresponding to olfaction; thus the smell of strawberries and the more specific memory of the strawberry-tart-aroma-of-summer-vacation would be located in the same area.

Researchers don't yet know where memories reside which are not directly associated with the functioning of the senses. Where, for example, is the memory of a film scenario or a myth located? Besides, the theory of the localization of memory is itself disputed as much because of experimental inconsistencies as because of logical ones. Some scientists have mocked that theory's absurdity, calling it the "grandmother neuron theory": if the memory of my grandmother is located in a precise spot in my brain, is it susceptible to vanishing altogether like a blown fuse?

The number of questions currently unanswered by neurologists prompts the thought that memory is a phenomenon that becomes more complex as one investigates it. The experiments on live intelligence by the biologist Humberto R. Maturana add to the present puzzlement of positivists.[8] For example, one of the most popular theories, one which has supported the metaphor of the brain-computer for a long time, has to do with sight: the eye conceived as a photographic cell transmits coded information to the brain, which then interprets it and responds with another message ordering action. This theory accords with the current view of the nervous system (as an instrument whereby the organism gets information from the environment, a representation of the world to compute adequate response). However, Maturana's experiments on frogs suggest that the eye (and not the brain) of the frog "sees" the fly, recognizes it and orders the tongue to catch it without any "computation" by the brain. The image on the retina is enough to provoke the muscular contractions that move the tongue, the mouth, the neck, and the frog's entire body. This experiment can be direct evidence that the frog's behavior of catching the fly arises because of the nervous system's internal relations of activity without any reference to the metaphor of getting information from the environment represented within. The image of the frog's eye recognizing the fly and deciding to act without help from the brain-computer brings to my mind images of hands that play

Mozart or a breast that yearns for and "remembers" a nursing baby.

It's remarkable what little influence neurological research has had on psychotherapy, which is after all the great "memory cure." Therapy became Mnemosyne's refuge once we left oral culture and adopted a consciousness associated with literacy. Even the most scientifically obsessed mind does not believe that traumatic memories can be cured by a manipulation of cerebral neurons. The therapist's office is one of the rare places where we go to tell our stories; we are certain to find there someone who respects the subjective quality of our memory, since the therapeutic value of telling our stories lies in that very subjectivity. When a "therapeutic" tale concerns a whole group, we call it "myth" whose function is no longer simply to preserve memory in the form of a narrative but also to pass on its meaning for collective consciousness. Just as I tell my therapist stories to understand who I am and where I'm going, myth asks: who are we, what is our story, and what does it mean to us?

The memories which emerge from the therapeutic hour seem at first like ill-assorted fragments. Then it seems that these bits of string form a knot, a basic conflict that keeps coming back no matter how you approach it. As a patient of mine has already expressed it: "Whether I talk about my father, my mother, my son or my boss, whether I talk about the past, the present or plans for the future, I always come back to the same basic scene in which, like the child in the tale about the little match-girl, I am watching other people enjoying themselves through a window while I am outside, forlorn, shivering behind the bakery shop window, burning my last matches for a few moments of illusion and warmth." Myth recounts something which repeats itself; it organizes memory around a basic situation. Not just narration and remembering what happened, it's also a fundamental tale outside of time which tells about something that happened once, is happening now and will repeat itself, always different and always the same. Hesiod says of Mnemosyne that she has knowledge of "what is, what will be, what was." Memory the myth-maker weaves the fabric of our lives.

> Memory is the seamstress, and a capricious one at that. Memory runs her needle in and out, up and down, hither and thither. We know not what comes next, or what follows after. Thus the most

ordinary movement in the world, such as sitting down at a table and pulling the inkstand towards one, may agitate a thousand odd, disconnected fragments, now bright, now dim, hanging and bobbing and dipping and flaunting, like the underlinen of a family of fourteen on a line in a gale of wind. Instead of being a single, downright, bluff piece of work of which no man need feel ashamed, our commonest deeds are set about with a fluttering and flickering of wings, a rising and falling of lights.[9]

Psychoanalysis developed within a context of pathology: the repressed material that interests the psychoanalyst is usually traumatic in nature. Psychoanalysis has served as a refuge for Mnemosyne but at the expense of restricting her territory to the tragedies and suffering that justify the attention of a therapist. Does this mean we don't have anything to talk about once we're sprung from our misery? Must not we continue to express, to refine and pass on the story of our lives? One of the attractions of archetypal psychology is that it helps to release the "memory cure" from the therapeutic setting. It introduces us to the monsters, the heroes, the great mothers and the eternal children within us not just for therapeutic reasons (when the monsters are giving us a hard time), but to give us back a mythological perspective. Mnemosyne helps us escape from the medical model of illness and treatment.

The modern era invented psychoanalysis, the therapy of personal memory. That's at least one for Mnemosyne! But since we can't put all of humanity on the therapeutic couch, how shall we treat our collective memory? Mnemosyne is trapped in personal memory which blocks imagination. Memory more and more is restricted to accurate records and documented events, while each of us is left alone with private memories and the culture has no voice. What has replaced myth and epic and all that the ancient Greeks associated with Mnemosyne? Christian mythology? It used to, but since it is fixed by dogma we cannot invent or adapt or even reinterpret the mythology. There's a very restrictive copyright on Christian mythology, and the authors are dead; there won't be a revised edition. The executors of the will, the Pope and his theologians, allow no changes in the text. For example, even if a majority of the faithful were to decide that "something" must have gone on between Joseph and Mary, they wouldn't be able, as the pagans would have done, to invent a new episode in the conjugal tale of this mythical couple. Anyone who reinvents the tales is at once driven into heresy or paganism as was D. H. Lawrence with his story of a sensual Christ ("The Man Who Came Back"), or Jung with his book on Job, or Scorsese with his movie on Christ, or the feminists with their reinterpretation of Christianity in less sexist terms. Just to think the story further names one "anti-Christian."

What about the historical novel as a refuge for Mnemosyne? Yes, certainly, but the novel, with some exceptions, remains the work of one person. It doesn't approach the dimensions of a collective work like the myths and epics which were modified by the long line of generations recounting them. The novel presents us with mortal heroes and heroines who shape our mythologies, but they do not stay long enough on the stage: the characters who have shaped the imagination of one generation are unknown to the next (and sometimes to the other sex).

History? Most historians will tell you they write linear history; indeed, their objectifying method has to do with Apollo, or Saturn, or Kronos, not Mnemosyne. Objective history has the advantage of not needing to be reworked by each generation, for there's no need to review the fact that Napoleon's soldiers were cold in Russia. They were cold and it snowed a lot—that's a fact. Unless some contrary information presents itself, this fact remains a given that is added to the series of causes and effects constituting linear history. But the myth of the conquering hero which undergirds the entire venture and defeat of Napoleon in Russia, as well as our understanding of historical conquest, is constantly undergoing revision. There have been other campaigns and other conquests as burdened by snow and cold that did not collapse. For the linear historian, Napoleon failed to take account of the climate. But the linear historians have failed to take account of the inherent defeat in every heroic myth.

What about film? Advertising? Propaganda? Artists who work in these fields mythologize constantly: myths and archetypes are their daily bread. As they count on a shared background to move us, we can consider them as servants of Mnemosyne, along with therapists. They too sing Mnemosyne's song, but we tend not to hear it as her song. Perhaps we had no choice but to abandon Mnemosyne in order to get to the benefits of written culture. It was necessary, at least for a time, to forget subjective memory, to forget Mnemosyne.

Remembering Happiness

In high school my history teacher used to repeat that "happy nations have no history." I thought this was a shocking statement. Happy nations do, of course, have a history, but recounting the lives of nations, of families, of persons whom we call happy is a task for Mnemosyne and not for a historian who would want to start his book with an objective definition of "collective happiness" (much more difficult to define than "collective unhappiness," which is easily connected to horror, plague, war, natural cataclysms). There's no point in remembering dates and facts or analyzing documents or studying law codes and architectural and sociological factors if one is not gifted with Mnemosyne's voice to render the flavor of the happy event. One needs the singing voice of Mnemosyne and her daughters to reminisce about happy moments. Rather than looking like a history text, the final outcome has a complexity that this poem expresses well:

> The remembrance of a black cap warbler
>
> That picks the remembrance of cherries in June
>
> In bygone days of the cherry tree in the sun
>
> Meets on a branch the immediate bird
>
> That picks in the cherry tree of today.
>
> Of the two, the lighter vanishes before the other.
>
> Who sings? The living bird or the bird remembered?
>
> And who listens? The one who listened another summer?
>
> Or the one who believes he hears
>
> A warbler in March in a still bare tree
>
> Assailed by hail showers and no bird sings?[10]

Proust and Colette mastered the art of describing past moments of happiness. In their writings as well as in their lives, Memory takes on the same supranatural quality as grace in the Christian religion. Their memories are so sensually communicated that, for example, Proust's hypochondriac Aunt Leonie and the cook Francoise live in my memory as if they were part of my own family. These characters took their place in my mental universe a long time ago, and they are still there as "family." I first read Proust when I was eighteen. During the time I was passionately immersed in his work, the Sunday walks at Combray seemed more real than my own life. I walked the countryside, smelled the fragrance of the flowers along the road; I lived with the characters in Proust's nineteenth century, gracious and restricted, ordered and eccentric. I have as many memories of Aunt Leonie as I have of some of my "real" aunts. Even more, I cannot help seeing my bedridden mother-in-law through the character of Leonie; she is the archetype by which I have understood my mother-in-law's decision to stay in bed for the past fifteen years. Leonie's character is stronger than any explanation my in-law could give me.

Proust, of course, presents an exceptional case, a kind of Mnemosyne hero. A biography based on interviews with Céleste Albaret, housekeeper in Proust's apartment in Paris, tells how, when "Monsieur Marcel" was writing about a dish he had eaten several years before in a well-known Parisian restaurant, he would awake his chauffeur at midnight to go search out the same dish prepared by the same chef in the same restaurant.[11] When the chauffeur came back, Proust took only one mouthful and was disappointed, as he inevitably was each time he ordered petits fours from Rebatet, a brioche from Bourbonneux, a Bourdalou pear from Larue, a raspberry ice from the Ritz, jams from Tanrade or beer from Lipp. "It's strange, I thought it was better," he would say, and he'd go back to work on the memory of the taste as if, in the end, his memory was more precise and more delicious than the experience itself.

> Today I think he had these sudden cravings in those moments when he ran after the time he had lost, but lost as we say of paradise. And each craving was always linked to a particular supplier dating back to his youth or, in any case, to the time when he still lived with his

> parents, and naturally, all this was linked to his mother who took
> great care of her style of eating, and of living.[12]

His passion for the past is the opposite of the growth- and goal-
oriented ideal that marks the heroic ego, who thinks in terms of
progress and development. From childhood we train ourselves to
focus on a goal. Of course, to reach a goal one must focus on it.
But Mnemosyne looks back, inside, and down. There is no need to
travel to revisit the house of our childhood. It cannot be found in a
geographical place, only in ourselves, far deep instead of far away.
Literature teaches us this. Joyce, Virginia Woolf, Tolstoy and
especially Proust did not go back physically to places from their
past to remember that past. And Colette, who wrote so well about
her love for her mother Sido, did not care to visit the real Sido
when she was sick and dying.

Lou Andreas-Salomé wrote to Freud: "We have a recollection,
but we are reminiscence. Poetry is the continuation of what the
child had to sacrifice in order to grow up. Poetry is reminiscence
perfected."[13] That is why it is so difficult to write the history of
happy people. Poetry inevitably gets mixed up with history; retell-
ing always becomes reminiscing.

Can Memory Survive Literacy?

> A civilization of memory becomes totally amnesic
> under the influence of the most violent poison: the
> writings of a religion certain of the truth enclosed
> in a book: its very own.
>   Marcel Detienne, *L'Invention de la Mythologie*

In the days of oral culture, the voice was the collective metaphor
by which the Greeks imagined the ability to remember, a sacred
feminine voice which talked, sang, recited, whispered in the ear.
Oral refers less to words than to mouths; that is, it moves memory
into the body's way of remembering: dancing, cooking, knitting,
or swinging an ax. The emergence of literate culture has seen the
metaphor of the Voice (woman's voice, Goddess's voice) replaced
by the Book. When we ask memory a question, we imagine a big,
open history book in front of us rather than expecting a voice to

answer us. Research becomes a question addressed to the Big Book of the Universe rather than one addressed to divine voices.

When we think of memory as a book, or as archives, or data banks, we see information and recollections lined up in an orderly fashion somewhere. They're not presently available and have to be searched for. We have to "re-call" our memories. And what we call back into memory is more or less unconscious and unavailable as long as we don't return to it by an act of will. This linear idea of memory, fed by a determinist ego-oriented psychology, differs completely from the "unconsciousness" which characterizes oral cultures. Obviously, it's neither desirable nor possible to return to the "unconsciousness" of Homeric man. Consciousness, as it has developed in written cultures, carries with it an idea of individual freedom, a crucial distancing which we would hate to lose after working so hard to achieve it. But it is useful to be aware that we've been trained from school days to think of memory as a file box where the information necessary for a decision resides. Looking at the pieces of information contained in our "personal file," we then choose to act one way or another. No longer a Goddess, Memory is an instrument, a tool, a "servant of reason," a file clerk taking orders from the Apollonian ego.

The individual Greek who knew Homer by heart didn't have to "search his memory" to remember a certain passage; the words came effortlessly to his lips at the right moment as if a voice had whispered them to him, thanks to Mnemosyne. By contrast we need to rummage through our own archives in order to recite a poem by heart, having been trained to picture it scrolling out verse by verse as if written out in linear fashion in our heads. To know Homer, Shakespeare, Racine or Corneille by heart, without missing a line, is certainly impressive, but there is more, and it's this more that teachers fail to grasp when the task of memorization becomes useless and boring. The passages "learned by heart" should be available just as my native language is available, immediately and directly.[14] Once in Memory, the words become part of our substance. Even words we rarely use are there within reach, with no effort needed to bring them to awareness.

I had an uncle who knew in depth the writings of Blaise Pascal, and at every opportunity he inserted a quotation into the conversation. For example, to my cousin who complained about a disagreeable, condescending boss he said: "Even if you are a duke,

I do not necessarily esteem you, but it is necessary that I raise my hat to you."[15] Or, one day when dinner conversation turned to war and foreign policy he threw in: "Why do you kill me? What! do you not live on the other side of the water? If you lived on this side, my friend, I should be an assassin, and it would be unjust to slay you in this manner. But since you live on the other side, I am a hero, and it is just."[16] Since at that time I didn't grasp the connection between my cousin's boss and some duke, nor between war and the bit about neighbors separated by a stretch of water, I saw my uncle as a kindly monologuist living in a world apart. But the others understood and appreciated his offerings either because they knew Pascal or because they knew my uncle. He had learnt Pascal "by heart" in the way the ancient Greeks learned Homer, except that he never quite found an audience at his level, whereas the Greeks could speak to each other through Homer, a shared reference point, a shared symbolic language.

Here we find a definition of community which derives less from functional interactions and communications than from shared memory. A reference to an extremely well-known situation can be analogous to the comments of a therapist who points out a situation well-known to his patient. He is referring to the archetypal quality of a given story, saying: there is this theme again.

The idea of reciting a whole book or rereading it a hundred times and learning it by heart is absurd in the context of a literate culture: why memorize it if it's in the book? A student who doesn't learn speed-reading and who doesn't keep up with the literature will not move ahead to make it in the academic scene. Few people still talk to each other as Proust's mother and grandmother sometimes did. Both women knew the letters of Madame la Marquise de Sévigné by heart, and the grandmother would at times scold her daughter by reciting passages from the noted marquise. If my uncle and these two nineteenth-century women could enjoy their literary culture in a way that recalls oral transmission and associative memory, perhaps we can too. Nothing prevents us from holding on to Mnemosyne, along with and in addition to scientific culture.

Jack Goody studied the characteristics of a culture passing from the oral to the written mode.[17] He maintains, contrary to rather widespread opinion, that a society in the process of acquiring writing is in no hurry to write down its great oral epics:

Gilgamesh, the *Iliad* and the Bible were only belatedly put into writing. Writing slips into a culture through calculations and lists: the first task of written memory was to set up lists of state debtors, pensioned priests and ownership of properties. Later the intellectuals set up categories, cataloging four-legged animals or fruit-bearing trees—the beginning of methodical thought. In an oral culture it would seem completely absurd to draw up such lists, whereas we do it spontaneously. When we want to acquaint a child with the animal world, he naturally leafs through an illustrated book where all the animals are classified by species and labeled by name; "this is a cat, this is a dog, this is a bird" comes from such a classifying thought process. At the zoo we wouldn't fail to read to the child the plaque which says the lion is a carnivorous mammal which lives on the plains. In an oral culture a parent's introduction of the animal world would draw on the archetypal qualities of each animal, linking it to a story instead of a category.

At the end of the nineteenth century Hermann Ebbinghaus invented his famous list of "meaningless syllables" to measure memory.[18] He made his subjects learn lists of sounds (bu-li-po, co-la-di, vi-to-du) to measure their ability to retain. The Greeks of Homeric epic would certainly have considered Ebbinghaus's principle crazy, that all the material used must be devoid of meaning. What exactly is measured? Certainly not the power of Mnemosyne! Not that the Greeks would have been incapable of such performances. In the *Iliad* there are "catalogues," long lists of warriors and complex genealogies requiring a stellar performance on the part of the storyteller.[19] But the storyteller, in order to remember them all, tried hard to do the opposite of what Ebbinghaus proposed: he transformed them in a way that produced meaning, associations and images. He gave them rhythm, sang them, rhymed them. Cyrus knew the name of every man in his army, Scipion could name all the Roman citizens, and Mithridates knew the twenty-two languages of his kingdom, but none of these would have had any patience with Ebbinghaus's nonsense syllables. Their performance says as much about their concept of leadership as about their prodigious feats of memory.[20]

But Ebbinghaus was at the origin of an important series of experiments in psychology and of a concept of memory which have made us forget Mnemosyne. Not until the Gestalt school did psychologists emphasize that memory must necessarily adjust, distort and transform recollections to serve human personality in an environment that is both complex and changing. From the 1960s on, molecular biology—by bringing together in one approach the new knowledge in neurology, genetics, physics, microbiology, chemistry and biochemistry—stole the show from experimental psychology in the area of memory studies.

Herodotus and Thucydides, the founders of the discipline called history, started from the principle that history begins where myth ends, thereby focusing on facts: written documents, found objects, verifiable observations, census figures, genealogies, the movement of armies, military strategies, measurable data and geographical realities. The cast of characters in their history included founding fathers, legislators, heads of state or armies—in short, those who "make history" by leaving tangible traces behind them: written laws, buildings, dynasties and empires.

This shift toward objectifying everything, which is one of demythification, has occupied us since classical times. It had to be done. Without the light of Apollo the history of thought would be very somber; rational qualities are hard to come by and subject to erosion by superstition and dogma. But once objective memory is given its due and we've confessed our commitment and admiration for the scientific method and historical discipline, we can still regret that an imperceptible shift has led Apollonian minds to infer that everything that isn't objective history is nonsense and that metaphorical thought is nothing but regression into the primitivism of pre-rational societies. As if the idea of development, growth, "progress" was the only perspective capable of protecting us from regression. To those who see the return to Greece as a reactionary move backward to a pre-scientific era, Alain De Benoist responds: "It has to do with linking again with what cannot be surpassed, and not with what is passé."[21]

Historians like to believe, and have us believe, that they're the best repositories of collective memory, the best guardians of culture. They write History, they don't "tell tall tales." Their kind of memory became an instrument, a tool, a "servant of reason," a file clerk for Apollonian ego-consciousness. They are after truth, not myth; facts, not fiction. They have forgotten that the Muses, sources of culture, were daughters of Mnemosyne before they were servants of Apollo. This journey from Goddess to servant status is reflected in the myths: the Muses, autonomous divinities in the oral culture, became second-class vis-à-vis Apollo, archetype of literacy. To be sure, a scientist needs a secretary to record observations with care more than he needs a Muse to whisper fanciful ideas in his ear. But she is there nevertheless, in the scientific theory which organizes facts and observations in a way that reflects the scientist's own favorite fiction. Being a Goddess, Memory can be put to sleep but never dies.

We can look at a culture without being forced to choose between science and imagination, storyteller and writer, my grandmother's stories and the library, the novel and the scientific journal. If we can bring together happily under one roof an artist son and an engineer daughter, a historian father and a psychologist mother, an aunt who reads horoscopes and Tarot cards, a neurologist cousin, a broker uncle, a grandmother who remembers and a French cousin who "talks like a book," we can certainly revive Mnemosyne without denying Apollo. I wish for a renaissance of the Gods and Goddesses of our "imaginary and inner Greece." I love Mnemosyne and dream of hearing her voice again, but I must admit I spend half my life reading authors whose classical erudition and intellectual rigor I admire. And in order to write this book I've had the help of my personal computer, without which I would bog down in disorder. But I also understand that Proust loved Mnemosyne so much that without her life could be "a matter of indifference" to him:

> I knew very well that my brain was a rich mineral basin where there was a vast area of extremely varied precious deposits. But would I have time to exploit them? I was the only person able to do this, for two reasons: with my death there would disappear, not only the only miner able to extract the minerals but the deposit itself; now, when I returned home presently a collision between the auto I took and another would suffice to destroy my body and to force my mind to abandon my new ideas for all time. And, by a strange coincidence, this rational fear of danger was developing in me at a time when the idea of death had been for only a short while a matter of indifference to me.[22]

He had the time to exploit the rich mineral basin of his memory and to extract the precious *Remembrance of Things Past*. But when this was finally completed, he lost interest in his actual life and died.

Computer Memory

> Our current concepts of cerebral processing and representation are all essentially computational (see, for example, David Marr's brilliant book, *Vision: A Computational Investigation of Visual Representation in Man*, 1982). And, as such, they are couched in terms of "schemata", "programmes", "algorithms", etc.
>
> But could schemata, programmes, algorithms alone provide for us the richly visionary, dramatic and musical quality of experience—that vivid personal quality which *makes* it "experience"?
>
> The answer is clearly, even passionately, "No!" Computational representations—even of the exquisite sophistication envisaged by Marr and Bernstein (the two greatest pioneers and thinkers in this realm)—could never, of themselves, constitute "iconic" representations, those representations which are the very thread and stuff of life.
>
> Oliver Sacks,
> *The Man Who Mistook His Wife for a Hat*

The metaphor of the computer has increasingly informed our notion of memory since the last war. The image of the library as world-memory-bank is fading as part of the modern epoch that comes to an end with the advent of computer culture. David Bolter notes that in 1960 a computer firm commissioned a feasibility study of a program that would include "all human knowledge" in a gigantic data base. The computer is preparing to swallow up the book, the data banks to swallow the libraries. Reflecting the arrogance of literate toward non-literate knowledge, this project cited by Bolter reduces "all human knowledge" to written knowledge.[23]

In a literate culture, knowledge and knowing how to get it are almost the same thing, a skill now so common it goes unnoticed. Who doesn't know alphabetical order, without which no access is possible to a telephone book or a dictionary? What university student hasn't learned the usefulness of a table of contents, an

index, a bibliography? An important part of our training consists
in learning where and how to find the right information, that
is, learning the access codes to book culture. Written memory
is there somewhere in a book, but it's not worth much if you
can't get to it. Sometimes we forget that there were no page
numbers at all on early books and, even earlier, no punctuation.
Imagine reading a textbook or scholarly work without pagination
or punctuation, notes, indexes, references! How much help we
have to read nowadays. A book today is also a map telling where
you are so you can't get lost in the overpowering imagination of
the text. Computer technology takes it one big step further by
literalizing the idea of the map as an icon on the screen.

But even though these procedures impose a linear order (alphabetical lists, numerical lists, etc.), the computer's capacity to
imitate "associative memory" allows for direct questioning of
the literate knowledge through our personal associations. Soon
we'll be able to consult the computer not merely through the keyboard but directly with the voice, mimicking even more strikingly
the procedures of associative memory within oral cultures: "Computer, computer, tell me all you know about the Greeks!" The
technology for replacing the keyboard with vocal interfaces is no
longer a problem, and the present delay in implementing it can
only be explained as a retarded reflex of our written culture.

The first specialists of artificial intelligence, of behaviorist
leanings, were blamed for having treated the more subtle qualities
of memory as if they didn't exist, basing their conception of computer memory on the outdated model of book memory. By contrast Douglas Hofstader[24] and Terry Winograd[25] think we must
study these associative subtleties of memory so computers can be
capable of making associations in an original manner, just as
human memory does, not simply holding and codifying information as a book can do. These computer utopians are hoping for
computers which can give valences to certain kinds of information, judging their importance for computer memory.[26] But despite
the extraordinary associative capacity of computer memory, and
even with great enthusiasm for computer utopia, we can't take the
computer metaphor literally. No matter how "personalized" and
"contextualized" it becomes, the voice speaking to me through
a computer won't be any more "personal" than Mnemosyne is
"truly alive," taking her breakfast of ambrosia every morning in

her Olympian retreat. When the specialists of artificial intelligence use the idea of "context," it can only be meant as analogy, because in order to grasp an emotional context one must live it or at least feel it through empathy or sympathy. Henri Van Lier, a Belgian anthropologist, can help us delineate the fundamental difference between computer memory (functions) and Mnemosyne (presences).

> I can only perceive presence in a subtle experience called *communion* whereas *functionings* are the very object of simple communication. It is noteworthy that we distinguish between communion and communication, sometimes union ("love is a union of spirits" says Corneille). Functionings are what science and technology usually detect. And this is the difficulty of human science.[27]

We can't help sharing the enthusiasm of Hofstader, Winograd and Bolter for the possibility of a memory which is no longer attached to the process of printing and marketing books. Computer memory allows us to modify, adapt, and personalize the screen text or the voice coming from the computer. It's like oral memory, easily adapted according to context, giving us back the mobility and adaptability that we lost with book culture. This "open book" that is constantly in process and ever in revision is no longer an unattainable fantasy, as Umberto Eco suggests.[28] It will change our conception of writing and communication.

Truth and Deception

Even if artificial intelligence attains the level of flexibility and refinement that these optimists predict, Mnemosyne still has a capacity that computer memory cannot provide, the capacity to lie. Only truth and untruth can be put into a computer, not half-truths, half-lies, or temporarily omitted truth—all of which create a certain misty quality, sometimes beneficent, sometimes not, which is needed to give our memories their living "moisture." If I ask my mother what I was like as a child, she can give a clever answer, lie a little, or half-consciously disguise the truth, having considered my present-day concerns and guessing why I ask the question. She can play down or amplify character traits which became dominant later on. Here Hermes is the ally of Mnemosyne. If a computer is programmed to lie, it can only say wrong things or randomly reverse certain affirmations, which is very different from a falsehood inspired by Hermes, the patron of liars.

Marcel Detienne studied the concept of Truth (Aletheia) in ancient Greece.[29] Aletheia is indistinguishable from Memory since she knows "what is, what will be, and what was," but she also cannot be distinguished from another Goddess, namely Deception. Rather than inevitable antagonists, Truth and Deception are two indispensable elements of knowledge, for all truth contains some mystery. The role of Deception is important to Truth because it supports ambiguity; it prevents any one belief from becoming so absolute that knowledge itself is threatened. The ancient Greeks knew the Gods didn't exist, were in fact a deception, but at the same time they knew they did exist because their power could be felt. It would weaken knowledge to eliminate the ambiguity that Deception provides.

But Deception is not a useful archetype for computer memory. Out of place here, it is best conceived in a relationship of complicity with Mnemosyne, Hermes and the other divinities who embrace ambiguity (Aphrodite, for example). Just as we wouldn't expect to hear Goddess Memory through the speaker of our computer, I think computer scientists would be wise not to take literally the metaphors based on the functioning of human, subjective, and "Mnemosynian" memory. Everyone to his own territory!

Confusion among the three memories—oral, literate, computer—may make us lose Mnemosyne once again, this time because we thought we'd found her in the associative quality of computers, not because we thought we didn't need her, as in book culture. "Forget your grandmother; just ask the computer that has your complete medical, psychological, academic, sociological, historical, ideological file, everything from birth on!" Take yourself to a nursing home, floppy grandmother; everything is on my hard disk!

A polytheistic viewpoint could give us a perspective on the three memories. It wouldn't combine them into a new entity pretending to be the whole of memory. It wouldn't deprive us of family stories or computer memory and lead us to depreciate the static quality of books in contrast to the dynamic quality of Mnemosyne. Specialists in artificial intelligence don't have to convince us that one kind of memory alone (instead of three) will do the trick, so that the "computer revolution" can take place. Differentiating among the three memories and appreciating their individual qualities seems to me a more interesting way to go than fusion and confusion of types. Conversing with a computer can certainly imitate human intelligence and give us an experience of quasi-oral communication. Hearing a voice, even a synthetic one, is perhaps more agreeable than the drumming of a keyboard. But we must preserve that portion of the wholly contextual word which sides with "presences" rather than "functions." After all, the Daughters of Mnemosyne, as Hesiod mentions, "sometimes tell the truth, sometimes lie."

As the nine Muses were her daughters, so the arts present this ambiguity of truth and illusion. Although the computer's associative memory theoretically can contain Mnemosyne's immensity, at the same time it sterilizes her by eliminating illusion. Deception is necessary to give birth to Mnemosyne's daughters, the arts.

Souvenir

As a conclusion to this part, I would like to share a personal memory, a souvenir, a reminiscence.

Under the influence of Mnemosyne I tried to remember the moment in my own life when the word *pagan* first held meaning for me. That took me way back into a world which now seems unbelievably old and anachronistic—and very different from what my life became later.

I was educated in a Catholic boarding school for wealthy girls. It was not where I belonged, since my family didn't come from that world. Beside the Rolls-Royces, the Bentleys, the chauffeur-driven Cadillacs that brought my friends back from their weekends at home, my carriage looked like a pumpkin resisting transformation by the fairies. My father had me driven back to school on Monday mornings by the oldest employee of his small firm, in a yellow truck which carried an electrician's aluminum ladder rattling along in the back. My pedigree and my social class were displayed in big letters on the truck's door: Oliver Paris, Electrical Contractor.

Of course, there were other daughters of businessmen at school: daughters of the cement king, the paper and pulp magnate, and the number-one used car dealer. There were also the daughters of pickled cucumbers, Cuban rum and Montreal gin. But they all stepped out of such impressive black cars that their origins in cement, paper, pickling or alcohol were forgotten, whereas I looked as if I were still stuck to the big rolls of electric wire, to yellow trucks and to workers in overalls. In front of the majestic entrance to the school, the others waited for the chauffeur to carry Mademoiselle's valise to the top of the marble staircase which led to the double oak doors. Their car engines were silent, and the chauffeurs were too, like the two bronze life-sized lions that flanked the monumental staircase. My chauffeur, who had attended my birth nine years before, was a cheerily nervous man, always in a hurry. He jammed on the brakes as he entered the courtyard, left the motor running (the loudest one imaginable), got out of the cab leaving the door open and the radio blaring, climbed up into the back of the pickup and from there handed down my dented suitcase. He quickly got back into the cab of the dusty truck and yelled to me over the noise of the radio, "Have a good week, kiddo!"

It was a snobbish world, and during my first years I suffered. But in time I found it natural to curtsy, to wear white gloves for the religion classes, to use a starched linen table napkin the size of a pillowcase and to roll it up after every meal in a silver ring engraved with my name, to eat soup without the slightest sound (placing the liquid "under the tongue, Mesdemoiselles, not on the tongue"), and to sit with my back straight, head high, as though I'd just swallowed a butter knife.

During the ten years I spent there I was happy when I could walk alone in the sumptuous gardens. There were an English garden, a French garden, and some wild undergrowth, and I learned to transfer the affection I could no longer express to my parents onto the trees, flowers and plants in these gardens. I made the most of the silent chapel, going there when no one else did, and its silence taught me how to meditate. I loved the library most of all, a sanctuary of books behind glass in cabinets made of dark oak. Almost all the books—and there were magnificent collections there—were displayed behind beveled glass panels that sparkled. (Sentimental novels, the most in demand, which the librarian considered unworthy of glass cabinets, were placed near the door, like rotting fruit that the grocer picks from the stand so as not to spoil the others.) I remember the moment, a moment of initiation for me, when the old librarian-Mother, seated in her wing chair between the window and the potted fern, silently and solemnly pointed to the drawer where the key to the glassed cabinets was kept, thus opening up a world for me, a world in which I took refuge for the next ten years.

In time I made friends, and I ended up with the respect of the worst snobs, not because of my fortune (which did not exist) but because I developed some academic skills that were useful to them at exam time. If you have no money in that milieu, you have to find other ways to be forgiven.

I was therefore mortified to learn, three years after my arrival (I was then twelve), that the Mother Superior, an admirable woman whom I considered a Saint because she was so fair and straightforward, hadn't chosen me to be part of a select little group. This group was to meet to discuss "Christian spirituality" with the new chaplain, a deep-voiced young man with whom we were all in love. I had been told that my manners were impeccable (bad manners could wipe out all spiritual merit), and I had assumed that my academic record had made up for the yellow truck of my origins. Furthermore, the sacristan sister had adopted me as her assistant; it was my job in the fall and spring to make bouquets for the chapel with the flowers I gathered in the garden while the others were in study hall. Weren't these bouquets and my frequent presence in the chapel enough proof of my spirituality? What more did Mother Superior want! I asked why I had been excluded, and the Reverend Mother called me into her private salon where the rug was as thick as woods' moss.

On a low table, next to the silver teapot and the two cups of English porcelain, she had placed a paper I had written the previous month on the theme "To love God: what does that mean for me?" which had been assigned to all of us. I not only admired the Reverend Mother Superior, I loved her. She was intelligent, and she had studied theology at the university before entering the order. What's more, she was beautiful in a majestically corpulent way. She served tea and handed you your cup like it was holy communion. She was truly a Mother, and very Superior, and very much Reverential. I knew she would tell me the truth: "Mother, why am I judged unworthy of the spiritual circle?"

"My child, here is your tea. You may take off your gloves if you wish some petits fours. I've read and reread your dissertation. When you describe the pleasure you feel in preparing bouquets for the chapel, it seems it's not God to whom they're given that moves you but the flowers themselves. You say you love the Gregorian chant, the sun coming through the stained-glass windows, touching the shining oak floor of the chapel; you are exalted by the smell of incense, the processions, the rituals and religious art, but it is your sensuality that expresses itself in this way and not your spirituality. You write how moved you are to wear a special dress and a white veil for the month of Mary, how much you love to make splendid bouquets for the occasion, but it's not the Virgin you honor. It's nature that you glorify, including your body which you are happy to adorn for the ceremony. Your spirituality is pagan, my child, pagan. Even your love for the Virgin is pagan. There's nothing wrong with loving the Virgin Mary, but you make her into a Goddess and that too is pagan, for the Virgin is not a Goddess but a Saint. And that's why you cannot yet be included in the spiritual circle."

It was not said unkindly, more in the tone of a professor handing back a corrected paper. But that moment was decisive for me: she had just given me my faith, or at least she had named it. So then, I was a Pagan!

Still I felt I'd been told I was somehow primitive, even animal, that something in me was lacking. After drinking my tea and eating all but one of the petits fours, I thanked her, put on my white gloves and curtsied, realizing that religion had never been part of my home life. My father was an agnostic. Perhaps it was better for the new chaplain to start his group with some true Christians. I didn't want to risk being seen as defective there too. I knew I wasn't rich enough, but now I wasn't Christian enough. So I let the whole thing drop, somehow pleased to be called something as original as "Pagan." I still spent time alone in front of the Mater Admirabilis portrait that I loved so much, painted by one of the Mothers, a true artist and, from what I could then understand, a Pagan as well, for her painting of the Virgin Mary presented her more like a Goddess than a Saint. I went on gathering bouquets for the chapel and for the new chaplain too. He loved flowers so much and knew their names and seemed so pleased when I brought fresh bouquets into his study. Wasn't he another Pagan too in his love for flowers? Was I surrounded by Pagans, disguised as Christians?

The young, beautiful chaplain did all he could to be what he called "modern": he held confession in his office rather than in the confessional, and we didn't have to kneel. When he said mass in our chapel, he wore a vestment of creamy white wool handwoven by artisans and seamless as Christ's tunic was supposed to have been. His priestly vestments were plain and unadorned in contrast to those worn by parish priests, which were overlaid with gold and silver braid and seemed vulgar to me next to the simple beauty of the garments worn by our handsome priest. In his sermons he spoke of woman as a "repository of grace" and recited to us the Song of Songs in his movie-actor's voice—we were all bowled over. In his classes he talked about Femininity so poetically that during the break we all clustered around him, thanking him, complimenting him, telling him how much we "adored" his courses. A humble, intense person, cultivated and honest, he had dark, piercing eyes and a voice that resonated in my ears as the height of sensuality. Sometimes he took three or four of "his boarders" out for ice cream in his Volkswagen, and sometimes he lent us Chopin recordings or let us use his office for long telephone calls. He was the only masculine friend admitted into the everyday life of a small group of boarding students, and I, like the others, dreamed at night that he, dressed in his white wool vestment, laid his hands on my breasts.

But the changing times and our own adolescent crises finally penetrated with force the thick stone walls of the convent, which up to then had been content to remain in the nineteenth century. The chaplain could not stanch the hemorrhage of our faith. Intellectual curiosity, once stimulated, is not easily extinguished, and we wanted to understand the monstrous discovery of sexism. Overnight my friends and I began to question all the regressive, outdated values of that education, cutting our teeth by attacking the Christian faith during our religion courses with this young priest who had inspired our first shivers of desire. We became his lost sheep, his challenge, his favorites, as he took on the defense of the Church. Collecting the most sexist passages we could find in the Bible—which is extremely easy given such a large choice— we became the prosecutors bent on establishing proof of a sexism that insulted us. When we set down before him the worst passages (from St. Paul), it seemed he realized it was a lost cause; he discovered along with us what these passages held that was terrible for our gender. Breaking down, he said he was ashamed of St. Paul, ashamed of the sexism of the Catholic Church; he said he could never have adopted such a scornful attitude toward his mother, his sister, toward Woman. But how could he change the dogma? He was only a priest, not the Pope! He was sad.

When he realized that some of us were beginning to confess our sexual sins with many invented specifics, he called us together, his ten foolish virgins, and tearfully announced his resignation. He couldn't go on like this; he wanted to go on a mission somewhere to help people who suffered in their bodies. The souls of young girls were too complicated, and he was too young at twenty-five to be chaplain in a school for girls on the point of becoming women. "No point in tempting the devil, right?" he concluded. We consoled him as best we could and tried to reassure him: he had given us a solid moral base, we would be honorable citizens, through his kindness he had communicated to us something of Christian love. Christ was not the target of our indignation. Christ really hadn't had time, at thirty-three and with such a tragic fate, to know certain aspects of life. Like the priest, Christ remained a virgin; he hadn't had time, etc.

After reassuring him on the value of his teaching, we improvised a champagne party in his room, with the permission of the Mothers but without their presence. Only the ten lost sheep. We collected enough money among ourselves to present him with Baudelaire's complete works, which a cultivated man of his sort could not afford to miss. The day before his departure, on a beautiful June afternoon, I gathered all the flowers in the garden for him without asking permission of the gardener. The morning he said his farewell mass, the chapel was bedecked with flowers as for a wedding. There were several baskets in his office, his Volkswagen was covered with garlands, and we all wept like Mary Magdalenes.

After his departure, the existentialist philosophy that I had absorbed during school vacations—along with black coffee and jazz, Simone de Beauvoir's *The Second Sex* (which had just been published and was all the rage), and the work of her companion Jean-Paul Sartre—completed the process, and I became a rationalist, atheistic and liberal, like most of the intellectuals of my generation and like the rest of my family. I didn't hear the word *pagan* for many years, and I was never again tempted to seduce a man of the cloth, perhaps because I never met one as handsome, open and decent as our chaplain with the deep voice, a Dionysos clothed in vestments who strayed into a girls' convent thirty years ago.

Now this opening chapter of my life becomes a closing chapter of this essay in tribute to Mnemosyne. The facts, the events and the people are all true. But the feelings turn the facts into a fable, and so I believe that this little personal tale demonstrates Mnemosyne's voice and her method of mixing truth and illusion, fiction writing and biography.

NOTES

Dionysos

1. James Hillman, *The Myth of Analysis: Three Essays in Archetypal Psychology* (Evanston: Northwestern University Press, 1972).

2. Henri Jeanmaire, *Dionysius* (Paris: Payot, 1951).

3. Euripides, *The Bacchae*, trans. Charles Boer, in *An Anthology of Greek Tragedy* (Dallas: Spring Publications, Inc., 1983), ll. 136–42.

4. Michel Maffesoli, *L'Ombre de Dionysos: Contribution à une Sociologie de l'Orgie* (Paris: Méridiens, 1982).

5. Gilbert Durand, *Les Structures Anthropologiques de l'Imaginaire: Introduction à l'Archétypologie Générale* (Paris: Bordas, 1979). Durand uses the words *régime nocturne* which we translate by "night-mode."

6. Gordon Wasson, Carl Ruck, and Albert Hofmann, *The Road to Eleusis: Unveiling the Secret of the Mysteries* (New York: Harcourt Brace Jovanovich, 1978), p. 21.

7. Ibid.

8. Plutarch, in Edith Hamilton, *Mythology* (New York: Mentor Books, 1958), p. 62.

9. See Ronald D. Laing, *The Politics of Experience and the Bird of Paradise* (Harmondsworth: Penguin Books, 1967), and David Cooper, *Psychiatry and Anti-Psychiatry* (London: Tavistock Publication, 1967).

10. Some body therapies have specialized in one phase of psycho-corporal development: birth and rebirth to the point of making it a kind of repeatable initiation. I don't know what the guide at Eleusis would have thought of an initiate who turns up every year to be reborn, but I like to think he would have suggested that once one is born it's necessary to move on to live one's life.

11. Euripides, *The Bacchae*, ll. 1121–129.

12. Ibid., l. 1298 (my italics).

13. Jean-Jacques Wunenburger, *La Fête, le Jeu et le Sacré* (Paris: Editions Universitaires Jean Pierre Delarge, 1977).

14. Walter F. Otto, *The Homeric Gods* (London: Thames and Hudson, 1979).

15. Nor Hall, *Those Women* (Dallas: Spring Publications, Inc., 1988), p. 21.

16. Werner Jaeger, *The Theology of the Early Greek Philosophers* (New York: Oxford Paperbacks, 1967).

17. Maria Daraki, *Dionysos* (Paris: Arthaud, 1985).

18. Robin Lane Fox, *Pagans and Christians* (New York: Knopf, 1987).

19. Michel Foucault, *Histoire de la Folie* (Paris: Plon, 1961).

20. Simone de Beauvoir, *The Second Sex*, trans. and ed. H. M. Parshley (New York: A. Knopf, 1953).

21. Luce Irigaray, *This Sex Which Is Not One* (New York: Cornell University Press, 1985).

22. Robert Graves, *The White Goddess: A Historical Grammar of Poetic Myths* (London: Faber and Faber, 1952).

23. This inter-species maternal communication has a therapeutic quality. One of my physician friends who has treated several cases of psychological sterility told me that more than once his patients have become pregnant after watching their dog or cat produce babies.

24. Euripides, *The Bacchae*, ll. 215–32.

25. Ibid., ll. 263–64.

26. Ibid., ll. 510–15.

27. Hillman, *The Myth of Analysis*.

28. Luke 1:38 (my italics).

29. Jean Pierre Vernant, *Mythe et Tragédie en Grèce Ancienne*, vol. 2 (Paris: Editions la Découverte, 1986), p. 8.

30. Ibid., p. 21.

31. James Hillman, *Healing Fiction* (New York: Station Hill Press, 1983).

32. John Gardner, *The Art of Fiction: Notes on Craft for Young Writers* (New York: Vintage Books, 1985), p. 65. "No fiction can have real interest if the central character is not an agent struggling for his or her own goals but a victim, subject to the will of others. Failure to recognize that the central character must act, not simply be acted upon, is the single most common mistake in the fiction of beginners."

33. Hillman, *Healing Fiction*.

34. Irving Goffman, *The Presentation of Self in Everyday Life* (Harmondsworth: Penguin Books, 1969).

35. Vernant, *Mythe et Tragédie en Grèce Ancienne*, vol. 2, p. 250.

36. Carl Kerényi, "Man and Mask," in *Spiritual Disciplines*, Papers from the Eranos Yearbooks, vol. 4 (New York: Pantheon Books, 1960).

37. William Shakespeare, *All's Well That Ends Well*, III, 3, 7.

38. William Shakespeare, *King John*, II, 3, 7.

39. Ibid., III, 4, 132.

40. William Shakespeare, *King Lear*, IV, 3, 22.

41. Marcel Proust, *Remembrance of Things Past*, trans. Scott Moncrieff and Frederick Blossom, vol. 3, *The Guermantes Way* (New York: Random House, 1930).

42. Ibid., vol. 6, *The Sweet Cheat Gone*, p. 17.

43. Robert Linton, *The Cultural Background of Personality* (New York: Appleton Century, 1945). Linton was an anthropologist and one of the first to write about roles after G. H. Mead.

44. Gordon Allport, *Personality: A Psychological Interpretation* (New York: Holt, 1937).

45. Goffman, *The Presentation of Self*, p. 213: "Ceremonial rewards."

46. David Shapiro, for example, considers theatrical behavior to be a trait of the hysterical style. "He seems to feel like a character in this romance, a Cinderella or a heroic and dashing Don Juan. When we see hysterical histrionics, we can easily get the impression that the person is 'carried away' by his own theatrics, and, I believe, there is a truth in this idea. He does not seem rooted in a sense of his factual being and history, in firm convictions, and a sense of the factual, objective world. Instead, he is actually 'carried away' by the immediacy of his responses to and the ease with which his whole awareness is captured by vivid impressions, romantic provocations, transient moods of his own, or the fantasy characters that, for whatever reason, appeal to him." David Shapiro, *Neurotic Styles* (New York: Basic Books, 1965), p. 120.

Hermes

1. Douglas R. Hofstader, *Metamagical Themas: Questing for the Essence of Mind and Pattern* (New York: Bantam Books, 1986).

2. Terry Winograd and Fernando Flores, *Understanding Computers and Cognition* (Norwood, New Jersey: Ablex Publishing Corporation, 1986).

3. Hofstader, *Metamagical Themas*, p. 548.

4. *The Homeric Hymns*, trans. Charles Boer, 2d ed. (Dallas: Spring Publications, Inc., 1970), pp. 37–38. Hermes' speech to Zeus follows on pp. 44–45.

5. Norman O. Brown, *Hermes the Thief* (New York: Vintage Books, 1969).

6. *The Homeric Hymns*, pp. 29–30.

7. Ibid., p. 45.

8. Ibid., pp. 47–48.

9. Ibid., p. 51.

10. Ibid., p. 55.

11. Ibid., p. 54.

12. Homer *Iliad* 2. 281–316.

13. Homer *Iliad* 2. 65–100.

14. Ibid.

15. Homer *Iliad* 17. 485–523.

16. Homer *Iliad* 7. 460–95.

17. Thucydides *History of the Peloponnesian War* 6. 27.

18. Homer *Iliad* 24. 466–71.

19. *The Homeric Hymns*, p. 48.

20. Walter J. Ong, *Orality and Literacy* (New York: Methuen, 1982).

21. Jack Goody, *The Domestication of the Savage Mind* (Cambridge: Cambridge University Press, 1977).

22. Erick Havelock, *The Muses Learn to Write* (New Haven: Yale University Press, 1986).

23. Goody, *Domestication of the Savage Mind*.

24. Hesiod *Works and Days* (Penguin Classics), p. 27.

25. Ibid., p. 25.

26. Ibid.

27. Henri Michaux, *Qui Je Fus* (Paris: Gallimard, 1927): "C'est dans tout indifféremment que j'ai chance de trouver ce que je cherche puisque ce que je cherche je ne le sais pas."

28. *The Homeric Hymns*, pp. 19–21.

29. James Hillman, "Notes on Opportunism," in *Puer Papers*, ed. James Hillman (Dallas: Spring Publications, Inc., 1979).

30. *The Homeric Hymns*, pp. 19, 20.

31. Ibid., p. 25.

32. Plutarch *The Age of Alexander* 4.

33. Cf. Dan C. Noel, "Veiled Kabir: C. G. Jung's Phallic Self-Image," *Spring* 1974.

34. Carl G. Jung, *Essai d'Exploration de l'Inconscient* (Paris: Gonthier, 1964), p. 73.

35. Ibid.

36. Ibid., p. 74.

37. Rafael López-Pedraza, *Hermes and His Children* (Spring Publications, 1977).

38. Dr. Barnett, "The Computer and Clinical Judgment," *New England Journal of Medicine* (1982): 493–94.

39. *The Homeric Hymns*, p. 47.

40. Homer *Iliad* 5. 389–424.

41. The psychiatrist D. W. Winnicot describes the case of a young boy who is compulsively preoccupied by strings, ropes and lassos. Winnicot sees in this obsession a symbol of the boy's need to tie down the mother, to communicate with her. The boy is obsessed with strings because he would like to be linked and attached to the mother. D. W. Winnicot, *De la Pédiatrie à la Psychanalyse* (Paris: Payot, 1969).

42. The Goddess Charis, from whom the word *charisma* is derived, is very similar to Hermes and Aphrodite.

43. Maurice Druon, *Les Mémoires de Zeus* (Paris: Plon, 1963), p. 88.

44. Laurence Kahn, *Hermès Passe* (Paris: Maspero, 1978), p. 178.

45. "These too are doors, ways for the spirit to come in. The gaps in learning, the absences in remembering, the spottiness in systematic work especially in regard to time (appointments, schedules, deadlines) may be necessary for keeping open and available—and superior to the senex style of order. Puer integrity would mean never covering these holes, and so personality integration, when imagined by puer consciousness, always retains gaps and absences, unshielded." Hillman, "Notes on Opportunism," p. 154.

46. López-Pedraza, *Hermes and His Children*.

47. From a discussion among the members of the Société Francaise des Seizièmistes published in *Mercure à La Renaissance: Actes des Journées d'Etude des 4–5 octobre 1984* (Lille: Poitiers, 1988), pp. 156–57, we can read: "On the one side, there is the Trismegistus, and one must give him the long beard and the rabbinic robe, and on the other side there is the young God. Is the young God always called Mercury, and the other always called Hermes?" asks M. M. de la Ganranderie. To that question Guy Demerson answers: "the young one is not completely naked, he wears a short coat; the other one, the old one, is all wrapped

up in clothes." J. F. Maillard also points to the fact that there are two astrological signs related to Mercury: the Virgo (more spiritual and contemplative) and Gemini (trickster and instability). So the Trismegistus is not only Thrice-great but equally Thrice-old!

48. Dom Pernety, *Les Fables Egyptiennes et Grecques Devoilées* (1758; reprint ed., Paris: La Table d'Emeraude, 1982).

49. *The Homeric Hymns*, p. 59.

Goddess Memory

1. Cf. Frances A. Yates, *The Art of Memory* (London: Routledge and Kegan Paul, 1966).

2. Aristotle, "De Memoria et Reminiscentia," trans. Richard Sorabji, in *Aristotle on Memory* (London: Duckworth, 1972).

3. See the deep exploration and exhaustive exposition of the theories of memory by Edward S. Casey in his book *Remembering: A Phenomenological Study* (Bloomington and Indianapolis: Indiana University Press, 1987).

4. "In keeping with Aristotle's own primary bias, there emerged an entire tradition of what may be called 'passivism', in which remembering is reduced to a passive process of registering and storing incoming impressions. The passivist paradigm is still very much with us, whether it takes the form of a naive empiricism or of a sophisticated model of information processing. In fact, since Aristotle's position was first formulated, passivism has been the predominant, and typically the 'official' (i.e., the most respected and respectable), view of memory. On the other hand, and as a consequence of this very fact, there has grown up a countervailing tradition of 'activism' according to which memory involves the creative transformation of experience rather than its internalized reduplication in images or traces construed as copies. Echoes of activism are detectable in Plato and Aristotle themselves, especially in the shared conviction that recollection takes place as a search—a conviction still resounding in notions of 'rehearsal' and 'retrieval' as these have arisen in cognitive psychology." Casey, *Remembering*, p. 15.

5. Wilhelm Reich, *L'Analyse Caractérielle* (Paris: Payot, 1969).

6. Alexander Lowen, *Bioenergetics* (New York: Penguin Books, 1975).

7. Marcel Proust, *Remembrance of Things Past*, trans. C. K. Scott Moncrieff, vol. 1, *Swann's Way*, vol. 2, *Within a Budding Grove* (New York: Random House, 1954).

8. Humberto R. Maturana, *The Tree of Knowledge* (Boston and London: Shambhala, 1988).

9. Virginia Woolf, *Orlando* (London: Granada Publishing, 1977), p. 49.

10. Claude Roy, "Souvenir, que me veux-tu?" in *Le Voyage D'automne* (Paris: Gallimard, 1987). James Hillman translated the poem for this volume.

11. Céleste Albaret, *Monsieur Proust: Souvenirs Recueillis par G. Belmont* (Paris: Robert Laffont, 1973).

12. Ibid.

13. Lou Andreas-Salomé, *Lettre Ouverte à Freud*, trans. D. Miermont, Collection Points (Paris: Editions Seuil, 1983).

14. "Memory resides in the heart, for when it does not come from the heart, we have no more memory than a hare" (Marquise de Sévigné).

15. Blaise Pascal, *Discours sur la Condition des Grands*, second discourse.

16. Blaise Pascal, *Pensées: The Provincial Letters* (New York: Modern Library), section 5, "Justice and the reason of effects."

17. Jack Goody, *The Domestication of the Savage Mind* (Cambridge: Cambridge University Press, 1977).

18. Hermann Ebbinghaus first published his book on memory in 1885 (*Memory: A Contribution to Experimental Psychology*, trans. H. A. Ruger and C. E. Bussenius [New York: Dover, 1964]). He was strongly influenced by the research of a fellow German, Gustav Theodor Fechner, who introduced into experimental psychology diagrams inspired by physics.

19. For example in the *Iliad* some passages read like this: "Now of Boetians, first, were Peneleos, Leïtus leaders, Clonius, too, Prothoënor, and also Arcesilaüs; who so inhabited Hyria and likewise Aulis the rocky, Schoenus and Scolus as well and the myriad-ridged Eteonus, Graia, too, Mycalessus of wide lawns, also Thespeia; they who dwelt about Harma, Hesium, Yea and Erythrae, dwellers in Eleon too, and in Hyle and Peteon likewise, Ay, of Ocalea too, and Medeon's well-built city, Copae as well, Eutresis, and Thisbe haunted of pigeons; all they who Coroneia, and who Haliartus the grassy, all that Platae possessed, ay, they who inhabited Glisas, they that dwelt in the well-built city of Thebae the Lower, holy Onchestus as well, that glorious grove of Poseidon; they that vine-rich Arne possessed, yea, those that Mideia, Nisa the sacred as well, ay, uttermost-lying Anthedon. Two score galley and ten bore Troyward these—upon each one youth Boetian embarked, in number a hundred and twenty." *Iliad* 2, ll. 494–510.

Parallels can be found in Irish epics or what was once well-known in our culture—the genealogies in the Bible.

20. Nearer to us in time is the orchestral conductor Arturo Toscanini who knew by heart every note for every instrument in 100 operas and 250 symphonies.

21. Alain De Benoist, *Comment Peut-on être Païen?* (Paris: Albin Michel, 1981), p. 27.

22. Marcel Proust, *Remembrance of Things Past*, trans. C. K. Scott Moncrieff and Terence Kilmartin, vol. 7, *The Past Recaptured* (New York: Random House, 1930), p. 389.

23. David Bolter, *Turing's Man: Western Culture in the Computer Age* (Chapel Hill: The University of North Carolina Press, 1984).

24. Douglas R. Hofstader, *Metamagical Themas: Questing for the Essence of Mind and Pattern* (New York: Bantam Books, 1986).

25. Terry Winograd and Fernando Flores, *Understanding Computers and Cognition* (Norwood, New Jersey: Ablex Publishing Corporation, 1986).

26. I do not include here utopians such as Hans Moravec, director of the Robot Institute at Carnegie Mellon, who believes in the possibility of connecting an extremely powerful computer to the corpus callosum, the group of nerve fibers

between the two cerebral hemispheres. The computer would oversee the exchange of information between the two hemispheres and would teach itself to "think." This solution would be for Moravec the equivalent of Mnemosyne, if not of immortality.

27.   Henri Van Lier, "Entretiens de Jean Louis Laroche avec Henri Van Lier sur l'Anthropologie Fondamentale" (Montréal: unpublished communication, 1985).

28.   Umberto Eco, *Travels in Hyper Reality*, trans. William Weaver (New York: Harcourt Brace Jovanovich, 1986).

29.   Marcel Detienne, *Les Maîtres de Vérité dans la Grèce Archaïque*, Collection Fondations (Paris: Maspero, 1981).